MOUNTAIN ROUTE GUIDE

LAKE DISTRICT
& HOWGILL FELLS

Tim Woodcock

Dalesman

Dalesman Publishing Company
Stable Courtyard, Broughton Hall,
Skipton, North Yorkshire BD23 3AE

Front cover: High Street. Back cover: Langdale. Tim Woodcock

A British Library Cataloguing in Publication record
is available for this book

Locator map by Jeremy Ashcroft

ISBN 1 85568 156 0

Printed by Midas Printing (HK) Ltd

C-t-C territory near Scandal Beck in Ravenstonedale (Route 21) page 84

AUTHOR'S ACKNOWLEDGEMENTS

For info: Amos Doron (and everybody at KMB), Andy Stephenson (and everybody at Bike Treks), Chris Marley, Forest Enterprise, Graham Hodgson, John McKeever, John Mullett, John Pitchers, Lake District National Park, Mike Bonney, Pepper Bros., Phil Nelson to name but a few. Kit sponsors: Camel Bak, Chartech Aqua 3 maps, DNA MTB frames, High 5, Hope, Karrimor, Marzocchi, Middleburn, Oakley, Orange, Polaris, Rock Shox, Shimano, Timax MTB frames and USE.

PUBLISHER'S NOTE

DEDICATION

For Kay

About the author

Tim Woodcock has been researching mountain bike routes professionally since 1991. Although a latecomer to cycling — he took to mountain biking soon after his two teenage sons — his MTB pedigree is impressive with consistently high placings in the infamous International Polaris Challenge, two-day orienteering event.

Tim is a regular contributor to leading mountain bike magazines and his atmospheric landscape and architectural photographs have appeared in books, magazines and calendars the world over.

He lives in Somerset with his partner Kay and they have five children.

CONTENTS

THE RIDES

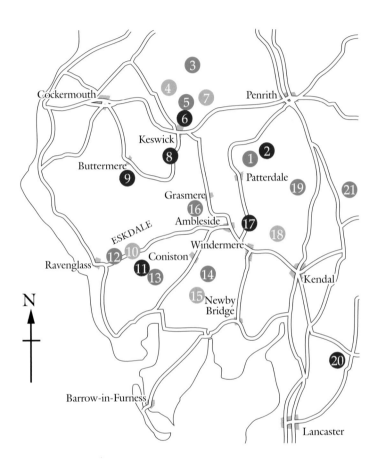

N

INTRODUCTION

The Lakeland District has the most challenging and entertaining off-road riding in England. It's also spectacular. So if you're looking for rides of a life-time, ones that are crammed with just about everything that's great about off-roading, this is the place to head for. Although there's a wealth of poten-tial plotted out on the map sorting choice routes from the chaff, fun rides for the novice from radical trails fit for an expert, isn't easy. Which is where this book comes in. Every route is planned and ridden with local, experienced mountain bikers. Those who know what to avoid, what to head for and where those classic off-road gems are hidden.

Within these covers are twenty-one loops and all, bar two, are within the boundaries of one of the most popular and beautiful National Parks in the world. Dramatic crags and ridges tower over placid lakes to create a concen-trated landscape that is Alpine in grandeur yet intimate in proportion. Whether you're tripping along the edge of High Street's 1000ft cliffs, skitter-ing down the Dash descent round the Back 'O Skiddaw, conquering a windswept Garburn Pass, dropping into the mountain fastness of Borrowdale or ambling along the farm tracks of Eskdale you'll find Lakeland riding is an intoxicating blend of awesome landscapes and entertaining terrain.

There's no doubt that off-roading in the fells of Cumbria is a unique experi-ence. It can be tough but then that's part of the challenge that pitting your wits, fitness and skills against the might of real mountain passes is about. "No pain, no gain" is an oft quoted adage that's particularly apt to off-road cycling. Even more so where mountains are concerned when pain, height-gain and enjoyment follow hard upon the heels of the other. There's precious little in the way of vistas when you're stuck in a valley bottom but up on the giddy heights of, say, The Calf, in the Howgills, a sumptuous rough 'n tum-ble tableau sweeps away from under your feet. It's breathtaking and imparts an exhilaration that's well worth the effort.

The trouble is that we're not all blessed with a fitness and strength that matches our appetite for height-gain. But the Lakes still come up trumps when it comes to routes for the tyro. There are plenty of short jaunts to enjoy — Eskdale, Ullswater, Grizedale Forest and Kentmere to name just a few — and most are low-level, easy to navigate and well-suited to the less seasoned rider.

Tim Woodcock
April 1999

PLANNING YOUR DAY

The routes

The routes described in this book are half-day and one day circular tours for off-road cyclists of all abilities. Of necessity 'day' is a very broad generalisation as the time of year, weather, ground conditions and the rider's abilities will determine actual ride time.

Although you will get a lot of fun and satisfaction riding a route for the first time invariably the best rides will be when you're more familiar with the terrain and are not reading and re-reading route directions.

Times

The time given for each route is based on the assumption that the riders are attempting a route matched to their capabilities, are familiar with route layout and there are no prolonged stops. If you are mixing two routes or just riding part of a route you can calculate ride times quite accurately; assume an average speed of about 3-4mph in winter and 6-8mph in summer with a penalty of 1- 2mph if the weather or ground conditions are bad. By habitually taking note of your estimated performance by comparison with your actual ride time you will soon get a good idea of how long your real 'day ride' can be.

Distance and height-gain

Rides of 20 miles or less can usually be slotted into a day with ease but rides of 30 miles and over need more careful scheduling. Although the length of each ride is an important factor don't be a slave to mileage. For the mountain biker height-gain is probably the most important, single determinant in the effort expended during a ride. As a rule of thumb rides making more than an average climb-rate of 1000ft/10 miles (300m/16km) will be strenuous — you need to be fit to really enjoy it! A day with more than 3500ft (1000m) of height-gain is going to be tough, especially in winter when daylight hours are few.

Grades

Each route has been given a grading according to its combined technical and physical demands:

FUN — Low/moderate technical demands; not strenuous; ideal beginner's route or winter ride when the weather's bad.

SPORT — Moderate technical demands; some hard cycling may be involved; ideal for those with some off-road experience or a 'quickie' for the fit.

EXPERT — Difficult/severe technical sections; strenuous riding; for the fit and experienced rider.

These grades are subjective and are relevant only to the routes in this book.

PLANNING

Maps

This guide book comes complete with OS maps and detailed instructions. If you want to explore the Lakes further the relevant Ordnance Survey 1:25000 Outdoor Leisure maps are: No 4 The English Lakes North West, No 5 The English Lakes North East, No 6 The English Lakes South West, No 7 The English Lakes South East and No 19 The Howgill Fells together with 1:25000 Pathfinders No 576 Caldbeck for the northernmost area and No 626 Broughton in Furness for the far south. The 1in Touring Map & Guide No 3 Lake District gives a useful overview to the whole area. OS Outdoor Leisure 1:25000 scale maps covering most of the routes are available laminated; this makes them less of a handful when it's windy. To protect this book on the trail carry it in an 'A5' size clear plastic, zipped document case and use a book-mark to tag the route you're on. Always carry a map folded to show the terrain you are crossing.

Hardware

I could wax lyrical on the benefits of lightweight titanium frames, tell you suspension is a must and how SPDs are essential for smooth power transfer. Then tell you how to remortgage the house to finance the purchasing of that 'must have everything' trick bit and frameset. But I won't. To begin with bike choice is a personal thing, fads and fashions change on a whim and providing it's sound any clunker of an MTB will do. Plus once you've remortgated your house what do you do for the ultimate upgrade machine? Having said that there are some pointers as to what makes a bike well suited to the task and what does not.

Use a good quality, reasonably light, proper MTB — 21 or more indexed gears — with alloy wheels, low gearing and a comfortable saddle. You're looking for a bike built for comfort, not speed; one with a relatively upright position so look for a medium length, high-rise stem and wide handlebars. We're talking several hundred pounds here but if you're serious about mountain biking it's worth it. Take a look at the mountain biking press for what's what then ask at a good mountain bike shop and buy the best that you can afford. If that's out of your budget then consider hiring one; there are plenty of hire outlets in the Lakes. Hiring is also a good way of 'balancing out' the hardware within a group. This is especially important if, for example, one of you has a clunker and the rest are riding lightweight titanium trickery decked out with suspension. A day-long 'mega' route will amplify the difference in ride quality; perhaps putting a downer on the whole outing. You should check your bike over before every ride, making sure it's fit to tackle the trails. Re-adjusting badly aligned brakes out on an exposed hillside, in winter, in the wet is a pain but a block slipping into the spokes could spell disaster! It's also worth having your machine serviced by a qualified mechanic at regular intervals.

Lakeland trails can be pretty bumpy so there are some bike accessories that will make your off-road excursions more enjoyable: some branded, good quality treads, with around a 2in carcass of new rubber for cushioning and grip — consult a good MTB bike shop for what's the latest trend in tyres and avoid cheap 'imitations' as they're usually made with low-grade compound and won't grip so well; on this terrain there's also a case for some sort of cushioning to negate the effects of riding cobbly cart track — full suspension is ideal but suspension forks coupled with a sprung seat-post work well.

Software

We're all aware of the weather's profound effect on our well-being — in the wet it's doom and gloom but once the sun pops out life's a party. It's all down to environment quality and it is clothing that determines the quality of our immediate environment. Except clothing choice is not decided on a whim of Nature. Kit yourself out with inappropriate gear that's been moth-balled in the wardrobe for the past five years and you're dressing up for a dose of doom and gloom. Uncomfortable. Take some time in selecting good quality kit and you'll be pleased to face whatever the weather throws at you. Even in summer controlling warmth is the vital element, versatility the name of the game. On top of Skiddaw it's a lot colder than down by Derwent Water; you can be shivering in the icy blast of a savage hailstorm while bikers by the lake are ambling along enjoying a summer's idyll.

Dress sense

Kitting out a mountain biker has proved to be one of the outdoor clothes designer's biggest challenges. It's a strenuous sport, generates loads of heat at peak activity then the loonies stand about mending punctures on a hillside with a wind-chill factor of $-10^{\circ}C$ and their body temperature plummets faster than the share prices on Black Monday. But designers are rising to the challenge and there's a stack of really good, MTB-specific gear to choose from.

The multi-layer principle is bandied about as the way to go — and it works — but there's always someone who has to swim against the tide and now there are several manufacturers producing single-layer, pile-lined kit. This is really late winter wear but can prove ideal for weight-saving freaks and experienced bikers out for a foul weather foray. So right from the start we're faced with a bewildering choice of kit, complicated by contrasting design convictions and all so technical that you need a science degree to discern what's what.

The best approach is to decide what you want the clothing to do. Ideally it should be light, have low bulk, be quick drying, resist the rampant sock syndrome, be easy to care for, fit well, feel comfortable and perform well. Whether it's to provide warmth, windproofing or water-resistance (unless you're a fair-weather cyclist you'll need clothing to perform all of these functions). Above all it has to wick — let your body lose moisture and 'breathe'. Under-layer clothing that soaks up water, sags like a wet flannel and dims the lights when the tumble dryer's turned on is useless. Likewise a top-layer that's built like a tent, flies like a kite and gives you your very own greenhouse effect is best left at home and used as a bin-liner. MTB and outdoor magazines regularly review cycling kit, back-issues are easily obtainable and their advice should at least put you on the right track.

Padded biking shorts are a must. There's no other item of clothing that will do so much for so little. Cut and style vary enormously and price does not necessarily reflect comfort and quality but generally the more panels they have the better, a seamless pad is less likely to chafe and for summer biking loose fit, touring shorts will keep you cooler. Female MTBers will find women's shorts far more comfortable than the equivalent man's version. Some folk are quite happy to bike without gloves but I invariably wipe out and grit my palms when I forget to put a pair on. Apart from protection for the accident prone padded mitts or gloves promote hands-on comfort levels, cushioning trail shock that may bruise you to your bones. On your feet there's nothing to beat a good pair of MTB boots. That's boots, not shoes. If you have SPDs check that your shoes have a deep, aggressive tread and that the cleats don't stand proud of the sole (pirouetting on a boulder on protruding cleats with a bike on your back isn't as funny as it looks!). Some SPDs also suffer from clogging when it gets really gloopy. And it can get seriously gloopy on some of the routes! There are alternatives to the ubiquitous SPD shoe such as light walking boots and mountaineering boots which grip well and give ankle support. Don't be tempted by making do with trainers unless you're good at grass skiing with a bike on your back. Even a modest grass bank can be insurmountable if your boots sport an inadequate sole.

Last, but definitely not least, wear a helmet! I'm not going to tread lightly round this recommendation for fear of upsetting MTBers who want to express some notion of freedom by going bare-headed. One day you'll crack your nut and like as not it'll result in a call-out for the mountain rescue team; they'll not be pleased to find you weren't wearing a skid-lid.

If you're riding in cold, wet weather then you'll need to add extra clothing, especially thermals (tights, tops and socks), full gloves, headband/snood and waterproof socks. In winter an extra-warm fleece/windproof top, for when you're caught in the open with an emergency repair, lined mitts and lined hood will also be necessary if you're tackling the high level routes. On the hardware side don't forget lights — all it needs is a couple of punctures and before you know it the evening's closed in!

Navigation

Your mapping is in this book. Just add a good quality compass on a neck cord and a weatherproof cycle computer — both of which you must be able to use with ease — and that's the pilot part sorted.

Survival kit

Mountain biking can be dangerous; a trivial accident above Boot or a major crash in Mosedale can quickly bring you down to a survival situation. A matter of life or death. Given the right kit, make the right decisions and you can turn crisis to drama, live to tell the tale and even laugh about it. Later. A good first aid kit and the knowledge to use it are essential. A basic kit should include antiseptic wipes, plasters, cohesive tape for wounds, triangular bandage, salt tablets for cramp and first aid instructions (first aid information, covering some of the common MTB emergencies, is given in the following section on Safety). You might very well be an accomplished first-aider. Whoever comes to your aid might not and they, not to mention you, will appreciate a set of instructions ready to hand. Survival gear — mini-torch, survival bag and whistle — can all be packed with the first aid kit. Pack it in a heavy-duty, zip-tie polythene bag.

Tools and spares

Quality doesn't come cheap but good tools are a godsend when you're in a fix so be prepared to pay for them. Most multi-tools will save weight on a tool-roll of separate bits but don't forget to check that your clever widget does all the whatsits on your bike.

TOOL KIT	Pump
	Tyre levers
	Full set of Allen keys
	Small, adjustable wrench
	Screwdriver (cross-head and flat)
	Chain-splitter
	Spoke key
BIKE SPARES	Inner tube
	Puncture repair kit
	Brake blocks
	Cable ties
TRAIL KIT	Compass
	Computer
	First aid kit
	Survival kit *(whistle, bag, torch)*
	Emergency food *(cereal bars etc.)*
	Seat pack, bar or bum bag
	(to keep emergency kit separated)

Once you've got all tools and spares together pack them tight and keep them handy — ready for the inevitable trail-side emergency.

Bag it

Fell walkers are a common sight on the trail as popular walking and biking routes regularly coincide — and many of them will be strolling along with pint-sized day-packs to take their kit. Take a leaf out of their book. Travel light — use a bum-bag or, on more adventurous winter outings, a small ruck-sack — about 20 litres capacity.

FELL RIDING

RIDE SAFE. RIDE LIGHT. Mountain bikers have run the gauntlet of being alienated by other countryside users since the word go but the sport of mountain biking is flourishing. Road improvements have dramatically shrunk the distance separating metropolis from isolated moor and mountain so our wilderness areas have witnessed a motorised invasion of leisure seekers. For a time hikers (and to a lesser extent hackers) had it pretty much to themselves but today many people have found that cycling intensifies their enjoyment of the countryside. A rump of ramblers see us as rivals, ill-informed environmentalists call us erosionists and farmers fear speeding bikes will frighten stock and uncaring cyclists will flatten crops.

The fact that it's a re-run of early rambler versus landowner conflicts makes no difference. Neither does the fact that the hoary old chestnut "cycle tyres cause serious erosion" is a proven misconception of some of our countryside companions. But we're here to stay and entrenched attitudes are already changing and this will come about more quickly if we ride responsibly.

Rights of Way

Although we've taken every care to try and ensure that the routes described in this book will keep your cycling within the law, at the very least the status of some sections will change. Plus, of course, you may get lost so it is as well to be sure of your Rights of Way.

Off-road cycling is permitted on bridleways, roads used as public paths (RUPPs), byways open to all traffic (BOATs), unclassified county roads (greenways) and designated cycle paths. Some sections of some routes are open to us with the landowner's consent and this permissive access may be revoked at any time. Cycling is not permitted on footpaths, open land or on pavements. Do not rely on signposts as reliable indicators of a route's status — local authorities do not always make correct use of BOAT (red), bridleway (blue) and footpath (yellow) waymarkers. If in doubt dismount. And remember, all land is owned by someone — even the remote moorland areas above the Lakes — and you must take care not to trespass. If a landowner asks that you leave it is in your best interests, no matter what the right and wrong of it may be, to acquiesce.

Of course you may be bowling along a bridleway when up pops a barbed wire fence and the way is barred. It's a tricky situation because your rights are wrapped in a woolly bit of rhetoric which says you can remove the obstacle sufficiently to get past if it is reasonably possible or make a short detour to get round it. The landowner can demand recompense if you cause any damage so clambering over it — often the instinctive reaction — is not a clever thing to do. This doesn't happen often but Rights of Way across farmland do get blocked, ploughed up, are over-planted or are stocked with dangerous animals. Farmers are supposed to provide signed, alternative routes but if you're in doubt don't traipse across regardless. Check with the owner and if you're still forced off the Right of Way report it to the local authority — The Lake District National Park or Cumbria County Council — who will take up the matter on your behalf.

Codes of conduct

You won't be the first to ride these routes so you will be treading in the tyre tracks of others. If they've careered along, forged furrows across fields, stampeded livestock, left gates gaping and created a trail of havoc and mayhem then you're not going to get a warm reception from the countryside community. Nor is anybody else who follows along unless you follow the Country and Off-road Codes:

- Enjoy the countryside and respect its life and work
- Guard against all risk of fire
- Fasten all gates
- Keep dogs under control
- Keep to Public Rights of Way across farmland
- Use gates and stiles to cross boundaries
- Leave livestock, crops and machinery alone
- Take your litter home
- Do not contaminate water
- Protect wild flora and fauna
- Take special care on country roads
- Make no unnecessary noise
- Cycle only on permitted Rights of Way
- Give way to horse riders and walkers
- Do not ride in such a manner that you are a danger to others
- Do not race
- Keep erosion to a minimum and do not skid
- Be courteous and considerate to others
- Be self-sufficient and make sure your bike is safe to ride
- Wear a helmet
- Follow a route marked on a map
- Follow the Country Code

They're not really a set of rules so much as guides that any responsible, thoughtful member of the mountain biking community would adopt without a second thought.

SAFETY

Three's company — better than two — but four's an ideal number outdoors in the wilds. With a party of three, when one gets badly hurt, one can go for help and the third can stay with the casualty. But ideally two should go for help, not one, which is why four is better. More and mountain bikers in a bunch can be an intimidating party on a narrow path.

Abilities, strength and stamina in any group will vary. Keep within the capacity of everyone, watch your pace and make sure everyone keeps within sight and sound of each other. But don't bunch up, especially on downhills, or there'll be some rear-end wipe-outs. And they can be real nasty! It's always a good idea to wait for stragglers at the top of climbs, at the bottom of tricky descents and at gates. It's in the nature of a strung out group to separate even further at such points so make sure that the young, eager pup out in front is aware of it.

One of the first signs of fatigue is when your normally ebullient companion rides quiet and persistently lags behind. Don't push it. Rest, drink, eat and keep warm exposure: may be just around the corner. Prevention is better than cure. Eat heartily a few hours before you set out and eat lots of carbohydrates. If you expect to be riding for more than a couple of hours then make full use of the various sports recovery drinks and carbo-loading preparations now available — after all you're just as deserving of their benefits as the athletes who advertise the stuff. Try not to ride for more than an hour without having some food — not as easy as it sounds — and drink regularly and drink plenty, before you get thirsty. Don't be over-confident when assessing how much trail should pass under your tyres during the day. Take into account the amount of height to be climbed — it's more important than mileage! The times given with each route are a guide and do not allow for stops. Even the terminally-fit will find that thirty-odd miles or about 4000ft of height-gain is about as much as they want to do in one day.

Weather

Out in the wilds weather will make or break a ride. Outside of mid-summer you can be subjected to sun, sleet, rain, wind, warmth, cold and calm all in the space of a day out in the Lakes. Maybe our highlands are minor mounds on the world map but it can be as bleak as Arctic tundra up on Cumbrian mountain tops when winter gets a grip. High Street might sound like an innocuous spot but, at 2740ft (830m), the exposed summit is often storm-lashed! It's easy to be lulled into a false sense of security, set out ill-informed and unprepared and end up the subject of a fell rescue operation. Get the most recent weather forecast and make a habit of catching the latest TV weather forecasts. They give a useful overview of what's coming.Three factors that strangers to the high moors often fail to take into account are altitude, wind and winter. As you climb temperature falls. Roughly speaking temperature falls one centigrade degree for every 100m gain in height ($3C^{\circ}$ per 1000ft) on a clear day, half that fall on a cloudy one. Wind-chill increases with wind strength. In a gentle to moderate breeze (force 3, about 10mph) wind-chill is about -5C°, about -10C° in a fresh, gusty breeze (force 5, about 20mph) and -15C° in a really strong wind (force 7, about 30mph).

It would be foolish to venture out onto the hill-tops if gale-force winds are forecast knowing that they'll be more ferocious on the higher fells. Take a furlough and explore one of the low-level routes. And be prepared to take an unplanned detour if the weather deteriorates badly whilst you're out.

Losing your way

Navigation can be tricky. Keeping on course depends on you, and preferably your companions as well, knowing your position at ALL times. Danger zones are forests, open moor and in poor visibility so take care to read the terrain correctly in these situations and make no assumptions about this or that trail being a 'main' route. One way of coping with poor visibility is to follow a compass bearing to the most distant visible marker, cycle to it, take another bearing on the next marker, cycle and so on. Most of the routes described take you along obvious tracks so you are more likely to feel lost than really be lost. But, despite our best endeavours to keep you on track, there's always a chance you might wander from the route. Nobody intends to get lost and it comes as a shock. Don't panic. Stop. Regroup. Make sure everybody's with you, then keep together and only then try to work out where you went wrong. Not too far back you'll have been sure of your position. Find it on the map.

Naturally you'll have been using your cycle computer to keep a log of point-to-point distances and it's a simple matter of reading the distance off, determining direction and that'll give you an approximate position. Forgotten to zero the trip distance at the last known point? Then estimate how long ago you were there and in which direction you have travelled during the elapsed time. Allowing for ground conditions, calculate how far you've cycled. Now check your surroundings and see if local landmarks coincide with your findings. If you're still unsure and visibility is poor then stay put until conditions improve.

In an ideal world three distinct landmarks should be recognised for you to be absolutely certain of your locality though, given two, you can still take compass bearings to position yourself. It goes without saying that correct use of the compass and trusting it, not your instincts, is vital. Many people get lost because they start navigating by guesswork instead of compass-work. A good GPS unit is an ideal companion to have on hand.

Fitness

Being fit is not just a question of muscle power. It's as much about recovery rate and in The Lake District some of the climbs are big. Legs that are quick to revive are not just an asset but, on longer routes, a necessity. Being in shape to take a mountain bike off-road in a landscape as rugged as this is takes time to develop. That's because fitness gains are made during the periods of rest between spells of activity. No rest and no gain. This also means that you can't significantly increase your fitness levels in an uninterrupted session of trail-blazing. You need time. So if you're treating yourself to an off-road spree slot in a couple of days furlough to allow that extra fitness to build.

Companions

A day riding rough stuff will be an enriched experience if you're in good company. A well-integrated team are much better able to overcome adversities with ease; even if it's a simple thing like bad weather. Not always so simple! But trail companions are notoriously tricky to choose and in the ups and downs betwixt the beginning and end of the day there will be stresses and strains. Off-roading is not all fun. On precipitous trails it's both difficult and demanding; add fatigue, perhaps a misread map and a ferocious wind and you've got a pretty good recipe for a falling out. Always distressing, discord can soon develop into dispute and that could be dangerous, in the wrong place at the wrong time. Choose companions carefully. It goes without saying that you should all get on but don't forget fitness. One mismatch — couch potato or fitness freak — in an otherwise well-balanced band of bikers will often lead to persistent friction and cast a shadow over the whole party.

Bike care

BEFORE RIDING: A routine check-up should include brake blocks, tyres, wheels and gears. It's a good idea to keep an eye on the chain, headset, stem, cranks and seat post. Don't forget to lube the chain.

AFTER RIDING: Treat your bike kindly and it'll be a reliable friend. At the end of a day hammering and being hammered on Cumbrian trails the last thing you want to do is bike maintenance but at the very least you should give it a quick wash, followed by a dose of water-displacer, oil on the chain then check it over. Do this right after a ride and you'll remember all those little mechanicals that have been niggling you during the ride plus wet mud washes off easily, dried mud is a lot harder to shift.

Trail-side fix fixers

BROKEN GEAR CABLES: You'll be left with a granny ring (front) or small sprocket (rear). Use the high/low adjusters to shift the mech to a middle gear.

TOTALLED REAR MECH: Split the chain and remove the mech entirely. Put the chain round the middle chain ring and a middle sprocket. Rejoin it, discarding sufficient links to take up slack, and you'll have a single-speed clunker.

SPLIT TYRE: Usually caused by a rubbing brake block. Stop at once. Deflate and remove tyre bead from the rim on the damaged side. Place a bank note behind the split on the inside of the tyre with a margin folded over the bead of the tyre so it'll be wedged against the rim when the tube's reinflated. Pump up and ride carefully.

TACCOED WHEEL: Remove the tyre then use brute force to push the offending bows back in line. Rest two apexes on opposite sides of the rim on two logs or rocks, the bow curving away from the contact point. Grab opposite sides of the rim and shove down. Only one log or rock handy? Then wedge a bowed out section of the wheel against it — or a tree — at an angle, rest the opposite sector on your knees or body and shove. Hard! No handy tree or boulder? Then whack the apex of a bow on the ground, refit the wheel, adjust with a spoke key, refit the tyre and ride very carefully. If you still have to disengage the brake in order to ride then it's probably better to leg it.

PUNCTURE — NO REPAIR KIT: Remove inner tube, cut/split across puncture and tie the resulting ends together. Partially inflate before replacing and refitting tyre.

Accident procedure

It's vital that at least one of the party is a qualified first aider. Ideally all of you should know the fundamentals of first aid. The British Red Cross, St John's Ambulance and St Andrew's Ambulance Societies all run courses.

It can't be over-emphasised that carrying a proper first aid kit with instructions and being a competent first aider is an essential part of accident procedure. But first aid instructions don't always cover the common illnesses and injuries associated with wild country mountain biking. These are given below:

HYPOTHERMIA / EXPOSURE (*The most common cause for rescue calls*)

Symptoms   Complaints of fatigue, cold, visual abnormalities
Lethargy, lack of interest
Cold, clammy skin, pale in colour
Slurred speech
Cramps
Clumsiness
Odd behaviour, out of character actions
Collapse and coma
Assume exposure if two or more of these symptoms are apparent and treat immediately

Action   Stop. Do not continue in the hope that you'll find shelter.
Shelter the patient. Wrap them in extra clothing and put them in the survival bag, with someone else if possible. If you have a sleeping bag then use it as an inner layer.
Warm the patient with bodily companionship and a warm drink if possible. Easily digested energy food can be given providing the patient is not too drowsy.
Cheer the patient up — low morale is a contributory factor. Be positive — the rest of the group will be feeling pretty worried.
Rest the patient for a prolonged period. If there's any

doubt about the patient's ability to recover then send for help.

Look for signs of exposure in other members of the party and signs of frostbite if conditions are severe.

Do not rub the patient to restore circulation.

Do not give alcohol — it may cause collapse.

Extreme cases sometimes stop breathing so be prepared to give mouth to mouth and if the patient does lose consciousness place them in the recovery position.

FROSTBITE *(Big descents after a long stop or fierce winds in winter are likely causes)*

Symptoms
Prickling pain
Numbness
Skin may discolour blue or white
Skin may feel hard

Action
Warm the affected area with additional body heat only. Extremities are the most commonly affected areas and can be placed in the armpit or crotch. The face can be smothered with dry, gloved hands.

Remove rings, watches, boots etc. to ensure free blood flow.

Return to civilisation and get the patient to hospital if at all possible or get help.

Do not rub the affected area.

Do not apply heat from an artificial source.

Do not use revitalised limb or the affected tissue will tear. Again seek medical help.

HEAT EXHAUSTION *(Common during periods of sustained effort)*

Symptoms
Pale, sweaty skin
Cramps
Complaints of dizziness, fatigue and headache
Rapid but weak pulse, shallow breathing
Fainting

Action
Shade the patient. Find a cool, shady spot and lay them down.

Cold drinks of water, slightly salted and with a little sugar if available, will soon aid recovery.

SEEK MEDICAL HELP.

HEAT-STROKE *(Severe heat exhaustion)*

Symptoms
Restlessness
Frequent passing of urine
Complaints of dizziness and headache
Hot, flushed, dry skin

Rapid, strong pulse

Fainting

Action   Cool patient quickly by laying them in the shade and removing their clothes.

Sponge their body with a cloth soaked in water until their body temperature drops and they appear to recover.

SEEK MEDICAL HELP IMMEDIATELY.

SHOCK *(Present in almost all cases of traumatic accidents)*

Symptoms   Pale and pallid skin, especially the lips

Rapid, weak pulse

Rapid, shallow breathing

Cold, sweaty skin

Complaints of dizziness and blurred vision

Restlessness

Yawning, pronounced sighing

Fainting

Action   Reassure the patient.

External bleeding or other injuries should be treated simultaneously.

Lay the patient down, protected from the ground and elements if it's cold, avoiding unnecessary movement. TURN their head to one side.

Raise their feet on a pile of clothes or small rucksack.

Loosen restrictive clothing.

Control body temperature with loose clothing.

SEEK MEDICAL HELP IMMEDIATELY.

DO NOT GIVE FOOD OR DRINK.

DO NOT APPLY HEAT FROM AN ARTIFICIAL SOURCE.

DISLOCATION (Elbow, shoulder and knee joints are most at risk)

Symptoms   Deformity of the joint, especially when compared to the joint on the opposite side of the body

Swelling around the joint

Lack of mobility

Severe pain associated with the joint

Action   Support the injured limb in a comfortable position. Use the triangular bandage for arm/shoulder dislocations when the patient can sit or stand, rolled up clothes for the leg.

SEEK MEDICAL HELP.

DO NOT try to manipulate the joint.

DO NOT MOVE the affected joint unnecessarily.

BROKEN COLLAR BONE *(Perhaps the most common MTB fracture)*

Symptoms Patient supports injured arm against the body
       Head inclined towards the injured shoulder
       Lack of mobility in the injured side
       Swelling at the front of injured shoulder

Action   Position arm of injured side with fingers up towards the opposite shoulder, palm flat against the body, so far as the patient will allow. Place soft padding between the upper arm and body.

Support the arm using the triangular bandage for an elevation sling off the good shoulder that encloses the elbow, forearm and hand.

Secure the arm against the body with a belt or rucksack strap that encircles the body.

SEEK MEDICAL HELP.

DO NOT MOVE the injured arm if it is too painful, support against the body in situ.

ROUTE DIRECTIONS, ABBREVIATIONS AND INSTRUCTIONS

Instructions are brief and to the point and follow a uniform format that is designed to give least hindrance on the trail.

The following abbreviations are used:

SO   straight on/over

L   left

R   right

LH   left-hand

RH   right-hand

Routes are split into small sections of usually less than 5.0m/8.7km that fall between natural stopping points such as gates and major junctions where it is convenient to zero the 'trip' distance on your cycle computer (resetting your computer at regular intervals reduces the divergence between your computer display and the distances given in the directions below).

Primary compass bearings are given in brackets where directions need further clarification and distances are given in miles and kilometres.

A straightforward route instruction for one of these point-to-point sections is described in one sentence as shown below:

"Go SO to gate into Cow Gill farm at 3.75m/6km."

Despite the improved quality of signing and waymarking some off-road routes are not easy to follow so additional information is attached. This may include through-junctions, major direction changes, fords, technical obstacles etc. together with their distance from the last point where you will have zeroed your trip distance. This additional information is provided as a running check on your point-to-point progress:

"...(on bridleway track at first), forking L (S) at T-junction at 0.7m/1.15km (onto technical singletrack) and following cairns from 2.3m/3.7km."

Placed together the complete instruction gives you the direction to set off in, running information, your destination (where you will next zero the computer's 'trip' distance) and its distance from you:

"Go SO (on bridleway track at first), forking L at T-junction at 0.7m/1.15km (onto technical singletrack) and following cairns from 2.3m/3.7km to gate into Cow Gill farm at 3.75m/6km."

SCALE

The maps used are based upon the Ordnance Survey 1:50 000 Landranger series which have been reduced by approximately 20 per cent. Each grid square represents 0.62miles/1km square.

The Landranger from which each map is taken is indicated at the start of each route.

NORTH EASTERN LAKELAND

Ullswater with Helvellyn beyond (Routes 1 & 2)

SPORT Route 1
ULLSWATER ROUND

DISTANCE
21 miles (34km)
HEIGHT-GAIN
1700ft (515m)
TIME
3hrs (dry)
4hrs (wet)
NAVIGATION
SKILLS
moderate
RIDE DIRECTION
clockwise

Outdoor Leisure 5
The English Lakes NE

One of my favourite low-level, off-season Lakeland rides this loop can be started from the Pooley Bridge end if need be. I prefer to start from the Brothers Water car park to get a warm-up along the undulating main road. Pleasant enough in the winter but best avoided in summer when it's best to do a 'there-and-back' on the east side of the lake. If you do that kick off with the Patterdale to Sandwick bridleway (in reverse to that detailed in the Martindale Common circuit).

Ullswater is one of Cumbria's most beautiful lakes. Set right beneath the dark and dramatic peaks of Helvellyn this slender ribbon of water is best seen from the eastern shore. And one of the best vantage points is from the helter-skelter bridleway that skirts around Barton Park woods. It's great riding but almost always wet and in winter the ice can build to glacial proportions. There's a short, sharp carry at the top of Boredale where a myriad of pathways criss-cross the Hause itself. Just skirt right, round a little hill then continue south down into Patterdale. This descent kicks off with a serious incline then degenerates into good rough track — a touch too rocky to concentrate on the magnificent views — which gets real cobbly towards the end.

❶ Start Cow Bridge car park (GR402133, off the A592 by Brothers Water). Turn L (N, towards Patterdale), forking R (on B5320, towards Pooley Bridge) at 10.5m/16.8km, turning R at T-junction (by Pooley Bridge church; optional start here) at 11.1m/17.75km and going SO X-roads soon after on unclassified road then bridleway track to waymarked X-roads at 12.5m/20km.

❷ Turn R, turning R by the Cockpit stone circle at 0.4m/0.6km, keeping R at T-junction by ford soon after on roller-coaster bridleway, keeping L at T-junction at 3.2m/5.1km, through Mellguards (please walk here), SO unclassified road at 3.5m/5.6km (immediately up steep grass bank), swinging L round spur and turning R at 4m/6.4km up to chapel at 4.1m/6.6km.

❸ Turn L on C-road, forking R at 100yds/90m (steep, twisty descent!), going SO (towards Boredale Head farm) at T-junction at 0.6m/0.9km, going through farm at 2m/3.2km, short carry at 3m/4.8km (pathways are confusing but your route continues S on the far side of Boredale Hause knoll), circling R then L on increasingly vague singletrack round knoll, zigzagging L/R (effectively SO) over singletrack at 3.3m/5.3km, over stream, swinging R on track soon after (tricky descent at first), going SO at track T-junction at 4.15m/6.6km, turning R by Hartsop at 5.1m/8.2km and turning R on A592 to start at 5.2m/8.4km.

EXPERT Route 2
MARTINDALE COMMON CIRCUIT

Off-road kicks off with an easy climb up to the Cockpit which is where the end-of-day descent comes in. But before that there's plenty fun-time off-roading mixed with a good measure of hard graft to enjoy. First up is the fun, roller-coaster run around Ullswater quickly followed by the unruly bit of singletrack from Sandwick to Patterdale. Hartsop is where the assault on High Street begins in earnest. About 1800ft up in a couple of miles.

There's no option but to put your head down and get on with the carry from Hayeswater Gill to the Angle Tarn path. It's about half-a-mile, height-gain is rapid so just concentrate on the reward — 10 miles of downhill pay-back! It's well worth taking the short excursion to bag the trig on High Street and enjoy the ride alongside the awesome space above Hayeswater. Dizzy! After that — bar a couple of short climbs — the descent to Pooley Bridge just goes on, and on... Watch out for front wheel grabbers in the boggy bits!

❶ Start Pooley Bridge (pay-and-display car park, GR470245) and turn L (through village) turning R at T-junction (by Pooley Bridge church) and going SO X-roads soon after on unclassified road then bridleway track to waymarked X-roads at 1.4m/2.2km.

❷ Turn R, turning R by the Cockpit

DISTANCE
25 miles (40km)
HEIGHT-GAIN
3850ft (1160m)
TIME
5hrs (dry)
6hrs (wet)
NAVIGATION
SKILLS
moderate
RIDE DIRECTION
anticlockwise

Outdoor Leisure 5
The English Lakes NE

An outstanding and virtually totally off-road route that must be one of the top ten in England. As with the Ullswater circuit you can start from either end of Ullswater but a Pooley Bridge beginning puts (a) the mostly downhill run off High Street as a fitting finale to an exciting day and (b) puts the technical trail from Sandwick at a time when you've the energy to enjoy it.

SPORT Route 1
ULLSWATER ROUND

EXPERT Route 2
MARTINDALE COMMON

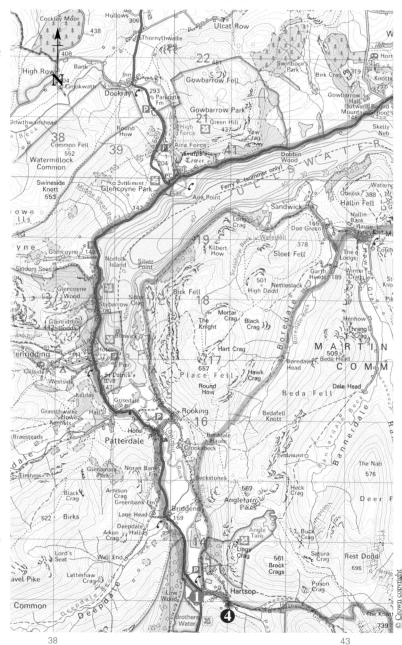

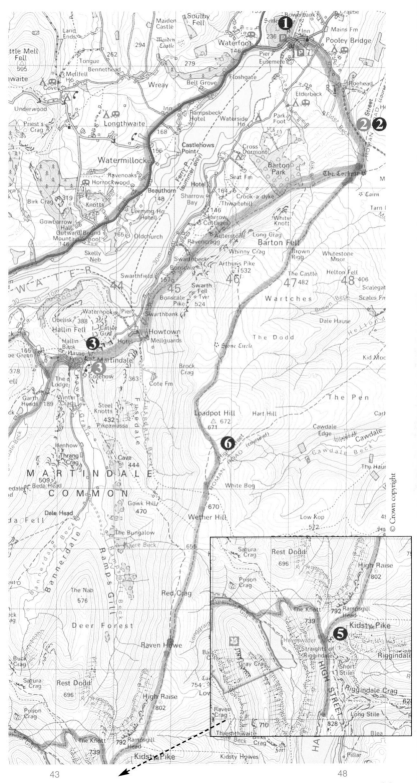

stone circle at 0.4m/0.6km, keeping R at T-junction by ford soon after (this is where you will come in on your return from High Street) on roller-coaster bridleway, keeping L at T-junction at 3.2m/5.1km, through Mellguards (please walk here), SO unclassified road at 3.5m/5.6km (immediately up steep grass bank), swinging L round spur and turning R at 4m/6.4km up to chapel at 4.1m/6.6km.

❸ Turn L on C-road, forking R at 100yds/90m (steep, twisty descent!), taking hairpin turn R at 0.6m/0.9km (towards Sandwick), forking L at 1.2m/1.9km up onto grassy bridleway (this bridleway is a popular ramble along twisty, technical singletrack — please remember the Off-road Code and give way to hikers) to follow Ullswater shoreline, keeping R at T-junction with bridleway path at 3.5m/5.6km (GR397183), through Side Farm (please walk) soon joining C-road turning L on A592 at 5.5m/8.8km and turning L at 7.4m/11.8km (towards Hartsop) to car park at 7.7m/12.3km.

❹ Go SO (through gate) on tarmac bridleway, forking R at 0.4m/0.6km to zigzag R/L over bridge (steep climb follows) to fork L at 1.1m/1.75km over river (fellside is criss-crossed by paths — your route circles L round N side of The Knott hillock 0.6m/1km E of you),

climb/carry E, swinging L at 1.6m/2.5km and turning R on obvious Angle Tarn–High Street track at 1.75m/2.8km to T-junction (50yds/50m before gap in wall) on Straights of Riggindale at 2.5m/4km.

OPTIONAL DETOUR UP ON TO HIGH STREET

— Go through gap and climb obvious bridleway along W side of High Street plateau (drop-off is on your R), turning L at 0.75m/1.2km (please be aware that there is no RoW on to High Street summit so please walk) to trig point at 0.8m/1.3km. Return by same route.

❺ Take hairpin turn L, keeping L at 0.4m/0.6km (just beyond rocky fell-top) on less obvious singletrack bridleway, going over Rampsgill and High Raise, passing through fence-line at 1.3m/2.1km then following fence past Red Crag Tarn, swinging R at 2.3m/3.7km, turning L after going through gap in wall at 2.6m/4.2km and turning R at 2.7m/4.3km on obvious singletrack to ruined chimney on Loadpot Hill at 4m/6.4km.

❻ Turn L (round W side of hill), keeping R at T-junction at 1.5m/2.4km and keeping L at 2m/3.2km and rejoining outbound route near Cockpit stone circle at 3.5m/5.6km to start at 5.4m/8.6km.

SPORT Route 3
CALDBECK FELLS

The multitude of mine tracks that criss-cross the Caldbeck Commons can confuse so, as this is a permissive route, please try to stay on course at all times. There are those that would love to see this welcome permissive access revoked! On the far side you're in territory that's little visited by mountain bikers but the riding, rough cart track in content, is great fun all the way round to the climb past Dash Falls. It should be rideable but I've yet to see anyone conquer it. On a clockwise run this is The Descent and one of the most exciting flyers in the Northern Lakes. Watch out for walkers though! From the YHA it's gently downhill to the end but the pathway's got rock-stoppers, peat pools, ruts and off-camber clambers to up the ante and add excitement. Some bits are a might boggy.

DISTANCE
21 miles (34km)
HEIGHT-GAIN
2740ft (830m)
TIME
3.5hrs (dry)
4.5hrs (wet)
NAVIGATION
SKILLS
moderate
RIDE DIRECTION
either way

Outdoor Leisure 4
The English Lakes NW
plus Pathfinder 576
Caldbeck

Outstanding loop round the Uldale and Caldbeck Fells featuring a long-awaited permissive bridleway linking Calebreck with Fell End. A real pot-pourri of prime-time biking that finishes with the entertaining singletrack bridleway down the Caldew valley.

❶ Start at Mosedale staggered X-roads (GR357323; parking at Mosedale Bridge and beside lane up Caldew valley). Head N, turning L at next T-junction at 1.5m/2.4km to finger-posted bridleway track near Calebreck farm 2.5m/4km. Turn L, on obvious mine track across Caldbeck Commons (signed Fell Side), swinging R at T-junction at 1.12m/1.8km, forking R at T-junction at 2.5m/4km, turning R down grass-track at T-junction at 2.7m/4.3km and turning R by marker post at 3.3m/5.25km to gate at Fell Side at 3.3m/5.3km.

❷ Go through gate, turning L on C-road, turning L up unclassified road (Dead End) at 1.8m/2.9km and keeping L on track at T-junction at 1.7m/2.75km to go through gate to C-road at Longlands farm at 3.4m/5.5km. Turn L, keeping L at T-

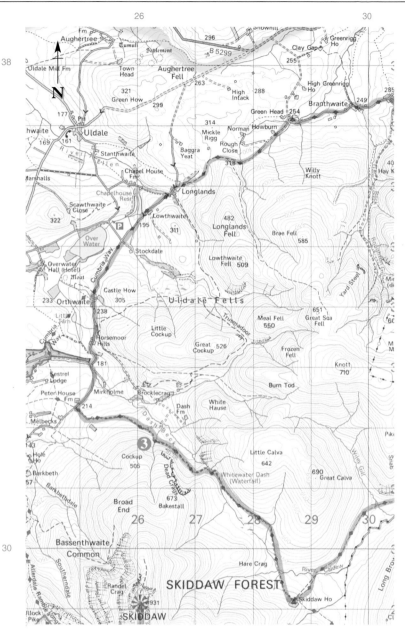

SPORT Route 3
CALDBECK FELLS

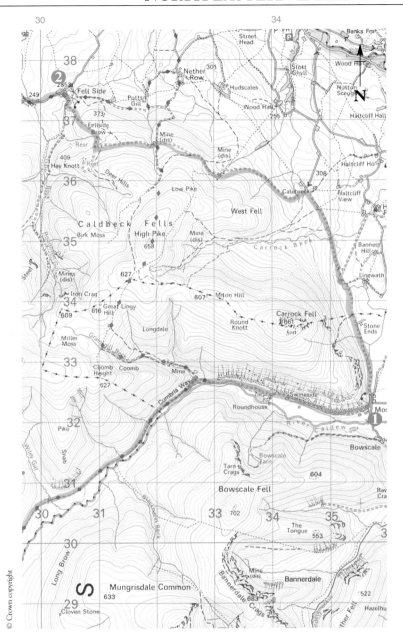

junctions at 0.75m/1.2km and 2.3m/3.7km, turning L through gate up tarmac bridleway at 2.8m/4.5km and forking R up bridleway track at 3.7m/5.9km to gate at 3.8m/6.1km.

❸ Go through gate, climbing past Whitewater Dash falls, to T-junc-tion with bridleway singletrack just before gate into Skiddaw YHA at 2.6m/4.2km. Turn L (next 0.3m/0.5km can be very gloopy) down singletrack to Mosedale, fork-ing R at T-junction at 2.5m/4km, joining C-road at 3.8m/6.1km down to start at 5.75m/9.2km.

FUN Route 4
BINSEY

DISTANCE
6 miles (10km)
HEIGHT-GAIN
675ft (205m)
TIME
1hr (dry)
1.5hrs (wet)
NAVIGATION SKILLS
easy
RIDE DIRECTION
anticlockwise

Outdoor Leisure 4
The English Lakes NW
plus Pathfinder 576
Caldbeck

Easy does it for a round trip of Binsey, Lakeland's northern-most knob of note; Whittas makes an ideal picnic spot if you're on a family fun run.

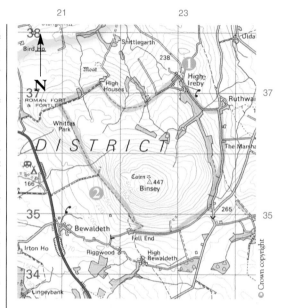

© Crown copyright

❶ Start at bridleway track/road T-junction (GR228371) in High Ireby (it's wide enough to park here) and head WSW on track, going through gate by stile at 0.5m/0.8km, immediately swinging L by wall and turning L at finger-posted T-junction at 1m/1.6km to T-junction with track at 1.5m/2.4km (easy to miss!). Take hairpin turn L, forking L up vague grass track at 50yds/50m, forking R down grass singletrack at T-junction on Whittas Park at 0.4m/0.6km (50yds/50m after broken wall), going SO singletrack junctions, through gated ford at 0.8m/1.3km and going SO track X-roads at 1m/1.6km to field gate at 1.3m/2.1km.

❷ Go through gate and climb L (no obvious trail), going through bridle-gate in field corner at 0.2m/0.3km, swinging R at 0.3m/0.5km down vague grass track and taking hairpin turn R at 0.5m/0.8km (soon after crossing fence line) to gate at Fell End. Go through gate, keeping L at T-junction with C-road, turning L at T-junction at 1m/1.6km, turning L at T-junction in Ruthwaite (signed High Ireby) at 2m/3.2km and turning L at 2.5m/4km back to start at 2.75m/4.4km.

SPORT Route 5
SKIDDAW ROUND

This loop packs in a pair of lung-busting, 1000ft climbs, wind-whistling descents and a couple of bites of technical singletrack with a great descent at the finish (best done in late evening in the summer season because it's a popular walk; otherwise avoid it by rejoining outbound route via the exhilarating Lonscale Fell bridleway or by keeping on the A591 into Keswick) and you'll have had a great couple of hours in the saddle. Can start at the northern end near Dash Farm.

DISTANCE
20 miles (33km)
HEIGHT-GAIN
2380ft (720m)
TIME
2.5hrs (dry)
3hrs (wet)
NAVIGATION
SKILLS
easy
RIDE DIRECTION
either way

Outdoor Leisure 4
The English Lakes
NW
plus Pathfinder 576
Caldbeck

This loop, known locally as the 'Skiddaw Round', tests trial skills to the limit.

❶ Start Bell Close car park in centre of Keswick (GR267235; Lakeland Pedlar cafe /bike shop here). Turn R (towards Ambleside) up A591 to X-roads at 100yds/90m then turn L (towards YHA), turning R on to rail-path by station at 0.5m/0.8km, rail-path zigzags L/R under A66 at 1.2m/1.9km, forking L over footbridge at 3.5m/5.6km and up alongside A66 to T-junction at 3.6m/5.75km. Turn L (towards Threlkeld), turning L (towards Blencathra Centre) at 2nd T-junction at 0.4m/0.6km, joining track by Blencathra Centre, crossing Glenderaterra Beck then turning R at singletrack T-junction at 3.6m/5.75km to gate just past Skiddaw House YHA at 4.7m/7.5km.

❷ Go SO (down track), steep zigzags (care! — walking route) at 1.7m/2.75km, rocky descent follows, going through gate at 2.5m/4km and keeping L on tarmac at 2.6m/4.1km (optional start point here; GR261320) to gated T-junction at 3.15m/5km. Turn L on C-road, keeping L at T-junction at 0.6m/1km (steep chicane!), keeping L on A591 soon after, forking L on C-road (towards Applethwaite) at

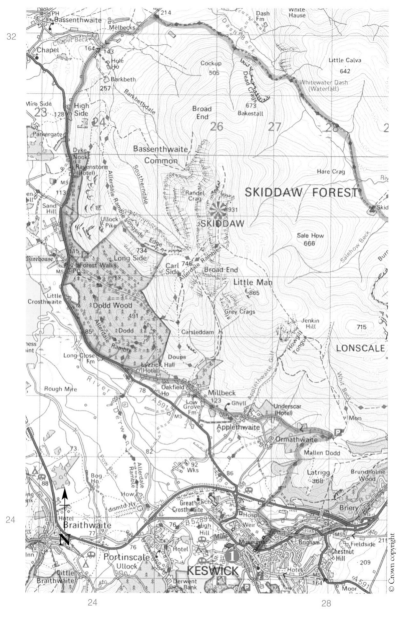

© Crown copyright

4.4m/7km, keeping L at T-junctions at 5.2m/8.3km, 5.5m/8.8km and 5.8m/9.25km and forking L (towards Underscar and Latrigg) at 5.9m/9.4km up to gated bridleway in car park at 6.75m/10.8km. NOTE: The next section is a popular walk so please ride with extra

SPORT Route 5
SKIDDAW ROUND

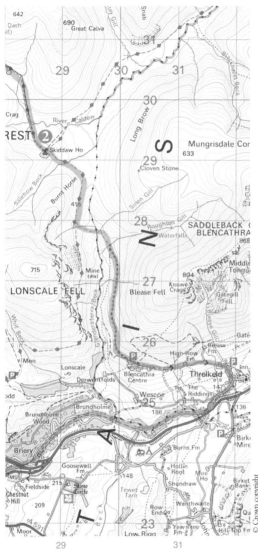

care. Turn R (W, towards
Keswick) on bridleway keeping R
at T-junctions at 0.8m/1.3km and
1m/1.6km, turning R on C-road in
Keswick, turning L on A591 soon
after and turning L at T-junction
at 1.9m/3km back to start at
2.3m/3.7km.

EXPERT Route 6
SKIDDAW MOUNTAIN

DISTANCE
10 miles (16km)
HEIGHT-GAIN
2890ft (875m)
TIME
3hrs (dry)
3.5hrs (wet)
NAVIGATION
SKILLS
easy
RIDE DIRECTION
there 'n back

Outdoor Leisure 4
The English Lakes NW

*Skiddaw's the name,
skidder's the game. All
up then it's all
dowwwwn! Five miles!
England's top-notch
descent is only worth
the work-out when
you're all but alone up
there because Skiddaw
is best enjoyed when
clear of other trail
users; if there are many
others about you'll end
up having to walk at
times. The descent
from Latrigg car park is
twisting and narrow so
it's best left until sunset;
an alternative, 'busy
time', ace return run is
to turn L after the
Monument and
descend Glenderaterra
valley to Keswick via
Blencathra Centre,
Threlkeld and along the
rail-path — it's almost
all downhill!*

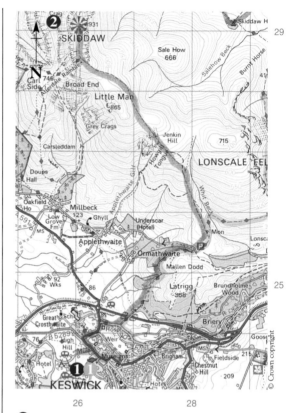

❶ Start Bell Close car park in centre of Keswick (GR267235; Lakeland Pedlar cafe /bike shop here). Turn L (towards town centre) on A591, turning R (towards Carlisle) at 0.4m/0.6km, turning R (towards station) at next T-junction, turning L (signed Skiddaw) up bridleway track at 0.9m/1.4km (popular walk, please ride carefully) and joining road and turning R past car park to go through gate at 2.3m/3.7km. Turn L (alongside footpath), forking L at singletrack T-junction at 0.15m/0.25km, past the Monument, forking R through gate at 1.9m/3km and over 'false' summit at 3m/4.8km to trig on Skiddaw summit at 3.2m/5.1km.

❷ Follow exact route back; if you want to avoid the steps on Jenkin Hill at 2.25m/3.6km fork L onto singletrack by fence and remember to keep R at T-junctions below Latrigg at 4m/6.4km and 4.2m/6.7km.

FUN Route 7
BLENCATHRA & LONSCALE CRAGS

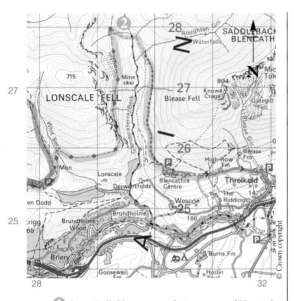

DISTANCE
12 miles (20km)
HEIGHT-GAIN
1190ft (360m)
TIME
1.5hrs (dry)
2hrs (wet)
NAVIGATION
SKILLS
easy
RIDE DIRECTION
either way

Outdoor Leisure 4
The English Lakes
NW

① Start Bell Close car park in centre of Keswick (GR267235; Lakeland Pedlar cafe/bike shop here). Turn R (towards Ambleside) up A591 to X-roads at 100yds/90m then turn L (towards YHA), turning R onto rail-path by station at 0.5m/0.8km; rail-path zigzags L/R under A66 at 1.2m/1.9km, forking L over footbridge at 3.5m/5.6km and up alongside A66 to T-junction at 3.6m/5.75km. Turn L (towards Threlkeld), turning L (towards Blencathra Centre) at 2nd T-junction at 0.4m/0.6km, joining track by Blencathra Centre (optional start from car park, GR302257) and crossing Glenderaterra Beck to go through gate at 3.4m/5.4km.

② Climb to singletrack T-junction at 0.25m/0.4km and turn L (slippery rocks round Lonscale Crags at 1.4m/2.2km) and going through LH gate at T-junction at 2.9m/4.6km to go through gate into Latrigg car-park at 3.1m/4.9km. NOTE: the following descent is twisting and narrow so please ride with care. Go SO, turning L through gate at 25yds/25m down bridleway (towards Keswick), keeping R at T-junctions at 0.8m/1.3km and 1m/1.6km, turning R on C-road in Keswick, turning L on A591 soon after and turning L at T-junction at 1.9m/3km back to start at 2.3m/3.7km.

A popular 'quickie' with bikers based in Keswick this little loop probably deserves a 'Sport' tag. The short slippery sliver of single-track round Lonscale Crags is 'doable' but dangerous and is a tad tricky for tyros. Ride clockwise if Keswick's bustling with tourists (walkers climbing up to Latrigg will seriously impair your downhill fun) when you can start from the car park by the Blencathra Centre.

NORTH WESTERN LAKELAND

A last look at Ennerdale before climbing to Whiteoak Moss (Route 9)

EXPERT Route 8
DERWENT WATER TOUR

<u>DISTANCE</u>
17 miles (27km)
<u>HEIGHT-GAIN</u>
3030ft (920m)
<u>TIME</u>
2.5hrs (dry)
3hrs (wet)
<u>NAVIGATION</u>
<u>SKILLS</u>
easy
<u>RIDE DIRECTION</u>
clockwise

Outdoor Leisure 4
The English Lakes
NW

*A circuit of Derwent
Water with just 6
miles (10km) off-
road doesn't sound
enticing but, believe
me, you'll appreciate
the metalled climbs
and welcome the
respite from the
100% concentration
demanded by
Borrowdale's boul-
der-strewn descents.
They ain't just
knuckle-jarring
gnarly, they're steep
and twisty too. Ride
every yard and you
can count yourself as
an elite expert.*

This is a short but sweet couple of hours in the heart of the Cumbrian mountains with spectacular scenery if you dare to look up! Best done out of season or as a summer's evening jaunt to avoid conflict with walkers.

❶ Start Bell Close car park in centre of Keswick (GR267235; Lakeland Pedlar cafe/bike shop here). Turn L (towards Cockermouth), soon turning L at round-about on B5289 (towards Seatoller along Derwent Water's shores) and forking L on C-road (towards Watendlath) at 2.4m/3.8km, climbing past Ashness Bridge (Surprise View at 3.3m/5.25km is worth a stop and look) up to Watendlath Farm (NT cafe here) at 5.0m/8km.

❷ Turn R (SW, across bridge), up rough bridleway (descent to Rosthwaite is steep with drop-offs, drainage runnels and paved sections; lethal when wet!), turning R through gate at 1.25m/2km and keeping R on meeting tarmac to B5289 at Rosthwaite at 1.5m/2.4km. Turn L (S), taking hairpin turn R on bridleway track (0.1m/0.15km past cattle-grid) at 2.1m/3.3km, passing sheepfold, forking L (up singletrack just past tree on RHS; easy to miss!) at 2.5m/4km to bridle-gate at 2.6m/4.2km.

❸ Go through (on obvious bridleway; highly technical at times), swinging L at T-junction by River Derwent at 2.1m/3.4km, keeping R at T-junction at 2.5m/4km and turning L in Grange at 2.8m/4.5km to T-junction with bridleway (marked by boulder near Manesty) at 3.6m/5.75km. Fork L (steep climb!), forking R (by woodland wall) on Cat Bells bridleway at 0.2m/0.3km, keeping L on C-road for 10yds/10m at 1m/1.6km and keeping L

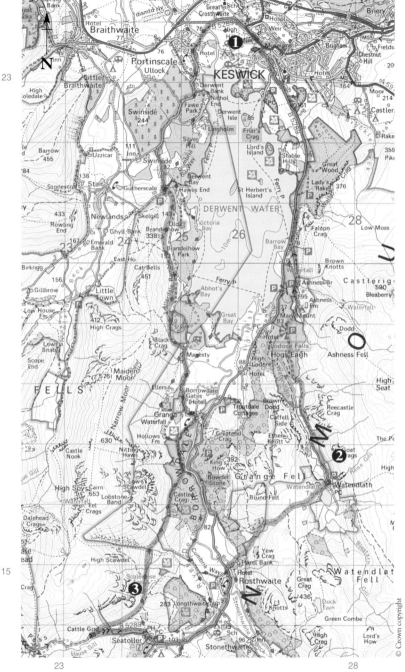

back on to bridleway to rejoin C-road at 2m/3.2km. Turn L (over cattle grid, towards Portinscale), forking R at 1.7m/2.75km (past hotel), across River Derwent on foot bridge and keeping R on B5289 soon after (there's a footpath alternative off to the R for a walk across fields to the town) back into Keswick and the start at 2.8m/4.5km.

© Crown copyright

EXPERT Route 9
HIGH STILE TOUR

DISTANCE
16 miles (26km)
HEIGHT-GAIN
2355ft (715m)
TIME
5hrs (dry)
6.5hrs (wet)
NAVIGATION
SKILLS
difficult
RIDE DIRECTION
clockwise

Outdoor Leisure 4
The English Lakes
NW

A tortuous climb, a rough run down into Ennerdale and a fire-road run west and soon you'll be whistling along the shore of Ennerdale Water.

Buttermere, in quiet times, has got to be one of the most beautiful spots in England. Turning to look down on it from the climb up Scarth Gap Pass gives you a good excuse to pause for breath. Then there's the run down into Ennerdale; water erosion wreaks havoc here so just how rideable it is will vary. This pine-plastered valley is bleak by comparison with Buttermere but the fire-road run west will make those knobblies hum. The desolate, marshy basin of Mosedale is traversed by a scarcely visible bridleway that fords Mosedale Beck — a bit of a torrent after rain; but don't worry if you lose your way just keep heading east and you'll soon find the singletrack down Scale Beck valley.

❶ Start Gatesgarth Farm car park (GR194150). Cross B5289 past farm (on bridleway track over Peggy's Bridge), through gate, climbing (push/carry) SO

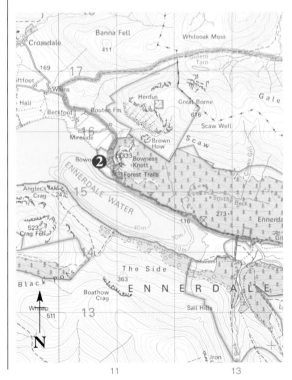

Scarth Gap Pass col at 1.4m/2.3km and following forest edge (down rough, stepped singletrack) to gated T-junction with track at 2.1m/3.3km. Turn R (into forest), keeping SO (mostly downhill) for 6m/9.6km through Ennerdale Forest to the barrier at Bowness Knott (car park and toilets here; optional start).

❷ Go SO (on C-road past Routen Farm), turning R (on gated bridle-way track) at 1.3m/2.1km and swinging R (E) after gate on to open moor at 1.6m/2.6km to climb to gate at 2.75m/4.4km. Go SO (E, passing 'Mountain Bikers Please Dismount' notice on Whiteoak Moss), soon swinging R alongside fence, going through bridle-gate at 0.6m/0.9km, immediately swinging L, fording Mosedale Beck at 0.8m/1.3km (can be difficult after

rain) and through bridle-gate immediately after on vague single-track (ESE, following lower slopes of Gale Fell) to go through gate in Scale Beck valley at 1.75m/2.8km (immediately after fording beck).

❸ Go SO (keeping N of beck on singletrack), forking R (over beck near sheepfolds) at 0.6m/0.9km, following Crummock Water's shore-line, over footbridge and turning L over Scale Bridge T-junction at 1.6m/2.6km to gate near Buttermere at 2.1m/3.3km (turn L into Buttermere village for cafe). Turn R (round Buttermere is popular walk so please ride with extra care), crossing footbridge at 0.3m/0.5km going SO path, imme-diately forking L (SE), exiting forest at 1.2m/1.9km and turning L through familiar gate at 1.9m/3km to Gatesgarth start at 2.1m/3.4km.

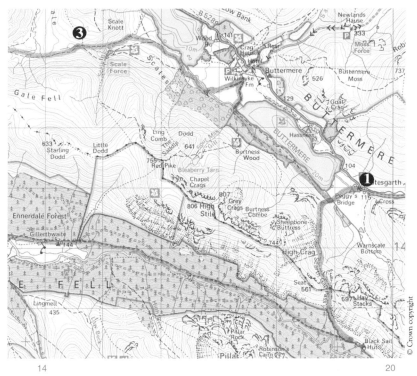

SOUTH WESTERN LAKELAND

Innocuous autumn evening at Boot, Eskdale? Not! (Route 12)

FUN Route 10
ESKDALE

DISTANCE
14 miles (22km)
HEIGHT-GAIN
265ft (80m)
TIME
1.5hrs (dry)
2hrs (wet)
NAVIGATION
SKILLS
moderate
RIDE DIRECTION
either way

Outdoor Leisure 6
The English Lakes
SW

An easy 'eight' up and down Eskdale's delightful tracks and lanes — ignore the tarmac and you're in for a great off-road return run

① Start Boot car park (GR173007). Turn R (down-dale), turning L (towards Ulpha) at T-junction at 1.8m/2.9km, turning R at 2.1m/3.4km onto finger-posted bridleway track, forking L at 3m/4.8km (soon after passing High Eskholme and signed Main Road) then following finger-posted route across links to gated T-junction with track at 3.4m/5.5km. Turn R, going SO X-roads at 0.3m/0.5km, turning L onto A595 (busy road!) soon after, turning L at T-junction (lay-by here for alternative start) after Muncaster Bridge at 1m/1.6km and turning L (towards Eskdale) at T-junction at 4.25m/6.8km to T-junction with bridleway track at 4.75m/7.6km (signed Boot).

② Fork R, going through RH gate at 0.5m/0.8km, turning R at T-junction at 1.3m/2.1km to gated, signed X-roads at 1.4m/2.2km. Go SO, crossing foot-bridge then turning R after going through gate at 0.15m/0.25km almost immediately swinging L, through ford then turning R at finger-posted T-junction at 0.4m/0.6km, immediately swinging L then keeping L on main track to gate at 1m/1.6km. Go SO, over foot-bridge, keeping L by Low Birker farm at 0.25m/0.4km, turning L at T-junction at 0.5m/0.8km onto unclassified road and turning L at T-junction soon after to start at 1.7m/2.75km.

EXPERT Route 11
ESKDALE/DUNNERDALE TOUR

The trek over Waberthwaite Fell used to be a nightmare to navigate but with a recent increase in traffic the route is a bit easier to follow though a 'trudge across the tundra' nevertheless. If you haven't got the right stuff don't go!

DISTANCE
30 miles (50km)
HEIGHT-GAIN
3370ft (1020m)
TIME
5.5hrs (dry)
7hrs (wet)
NAVIGATION SKILLS
difficult
RIDE DIRECTION
anticlockwise

Outdoor Leisure 6 The English Lakes SW

The full mountain bike experience with everything from forest fast-tracking to rock-hopping, endo-inducing singletrack.

❶ Start Boot car-park (GR173007). Turn L (up-dale), turning R (towards Penny Hill farm) at T-junction at 1m/1.6km, turning R immediately after bridge, keeping R past Low Birker farm, forking L down across ford at finger-posted T-junction at 2.3m/3.7km to gated X-roads at 2.6m/4.2km. Go SO (signed Forge Bridge), forking L at T-junction at 0.15m/0.25km, keeping R soon after, rocky drop at 0.9m/1.4km, going through gate at 1.1m/1.75km to C-road at 2.6m/4.2km. (NOTE: for short/bad weather version continue on road towards Ulpha, over Ulpha Fell into Dunnerdale then turn R for 0.5m/0.8km to rejoin route at para 4)

❷ Keep L, turning R at 0.25m/0.4km onto finger-posted bridleway track, forking L at 2.6m/4.2km (soon after passing High Eskholme and signed Main Road) then following finger-posted route across links to gated T-junction with track at 3.1m/5km. Turn R, going SO X-roads at 0.3m/0.5km, turning L onto A595 (busy road!) soon after, forking L onto C-road at 2.4m/3.9km in Broad Oak, turning L up Fell Lane at 3m/4.8km to go through gate on LH bend at 3.3m/5.3km. NOTE: next mile or so is confused by a myriad of 'trails'; you're heading for the bottom, the obvious 'Y-shaped' gully almost directly in front (ESE) of you; there the tyre tracks of others get more obvious. Go SO on track for

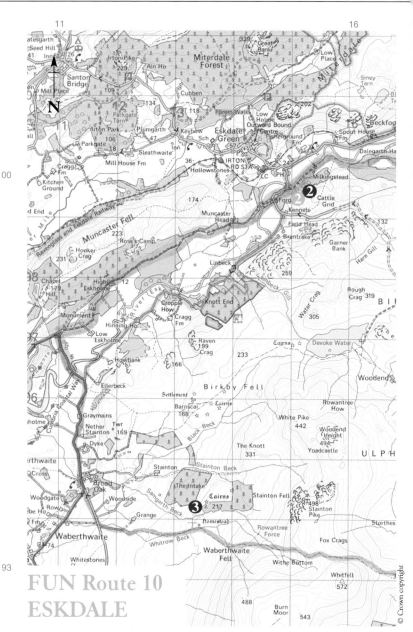

© Crown copyright

FUN Route 10
ESKDALE

EXPERT Route 11
ESKDALE/DUNNERDALE TOUR

100yds/90m, forking L down single-track, over ford into an area of cairns where route gets muddled at around 0.15m/0.25km so swing R

(E), crossing stream at 0.7m/1.15km and swinging L (NE) onto track with marker posts at 0.8m/1.3km to the 'homestead' (vague remains of

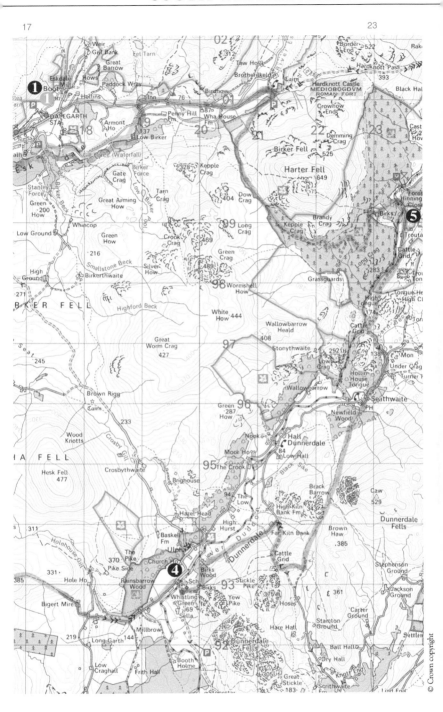

large, walled enclosure) at
1m/1.6km.

❸ Turn R (ESE, directly towards

the gully), forking L (E) up grass-
track at 0.4m/0.6km, fording
Rowan–Tree Gill at 1.15m/1.9km
then turning R by fence to corner

at 2.25m/3.6km. Go round corner for 100yds/90m then turn R (E, on vague singletrack) to Fox Crags cairn at 0.4m/0.6km, swinging R (ESE then E) across col, contouring round lower crags of Whitfell and swinging R on grass-track at around 0.75m/1.2km to go through gate at 1m/1.6km. Go SO on singletrack that slowly swings R and joins gated track at 0.6m/1km through Bigert Mire farm, turning R at T-junction with unclassified road at 1.2m/1.9km then turning L at T-junction soon after to T-junction by Ulpha Bridge at 2.5m/4km.

❹ NOTE: go SO to resupply at Ulpha PO 0.25m/0.4km away. Turn R, turning L at 0.12m/0.2km up bridleway drive, going through gate onto forest track at 0.25m/0.4km, forking R at T-junction at 0.6m/1km and turning R up C-road at Kiln Bank at 1.6m/2.6km to X-roads with bridleway on summit at 2.2m/3.5km. Turn L then immediately fork R (E) onto single-track bridleway, turning L (on track at first) at X-roads at 0.2m/0.3km, keeping L up bridleway at 0.3m/0.5km, soon alongside wall, keeping L at bridleway T-junction (in valley below Brock Barrow) at 1m/1.6km, turning R on C-road (Seathwaite, pub here) at 2.2m/3.5km to T-junction with bridleway at 4.6m/7.3km (NOTE: an alternative start/finish is Dunnerdale Forest car park 0.1m/0.15km further on).

❺ Turn L on bridleway drive past Birks, track takes hairpin turn L at 0.5m/0.8km then keeping on main track R at 0.9m/1.4km and 1.1m/1.75km to terminus with way-marker at 2m/3.2km. Go SO for push up rocky bridleway single-track, going through gate onto open fell at 0.4m/0.6km, swinging R soon after rocky drops (slippery when wet!) at 1.1m/1.75km, going through gates to C-road at 1.8m/2.9km and turning L back to start at 4.6m/7.4km.

SPORT Route 12
IRTON AND ESKDALE FELLS

❶ Start Boot car-park (GR173007). Turn L (up-dale), turning R (towards Penny Hill farm) at T-junction at 1m/1.6km, turning R immediately after bridge, keeping R past Low Birker farm, forking L down across ford at finger-posted T-junction at 2.3m/3.7km to gated X-roads at 2.6m/4.2km. Go SO (signed Forge Bridge), forking L at T-junction at 0.15m/0.25km, keeping R soon after, rocky drop at 0.9m/1.4km, going through gate at 1.1m/1.75km to C-road at 2.6m/4.2km. Turn R (towards Eskdale Green), turning R (towards school) at 1.2m/1.9km to track/bridle-way staggered X-roads at 2m/3.2km.

❷ Turn L, through gate, over foot-bridge then immediately swinging L, going SO all X-roads on tough climb with short carry at 0.6m/1km, going SO through gate at 1.1m/1.75km and going SO singletrack X-roads on top of Irton Fell (steep, stepped, soft descent — endos!) to bridle-gate at 1.5m/2.4km. Go SO, joining track briefly at 0.2m/0.3km then turning R down singletrack bridleway, going through field gate by tarn at 0.5m/0.8km and going SO (NNW) to bridle-gate to left of house at 0.6m/1km. Turn R onto C-road, zigzagging R/L at 0.12m/0.2km onto bridleway track (signed Buckbarrow), turning R through gate at 0.7m/1.15km (signed Buckbarrow), turning R at waymarked T-junction at 0.75m/1.2km, turning L at 0.9m/1.4km (signed Greendale) and keeping R then L at T-junctions at 1.2m/1.9km to C-road.

DISTANCE
14 miles (23km)
HEIGHT-GAIN
2000ft (610m)
TIME
3.5hrs (dry)
4.5hrs (wet)
NAVIGATION SKILLS
moderate
RIDE DIRECTION
clockwise

Outdoor Leisure 6 The English Lakes SW

Lots of real sweet off-roading tempered with a heavy-duty haul over Irton Fell but rewards come thick and fast on the descent to Boot. Arguably one of the best bits of technical riding in Western Cumbria.

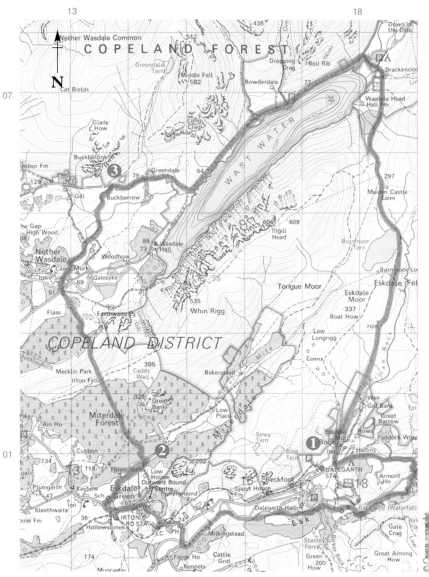

SPORT Route 12
IRTON AND ESKDALE

❸ Turn R, turning R at T-junction at 3.1m/5km (signed Boot), turning L at 3.25m/5.25km (signed Eskdale) and turning R past Brackenclose at signed T-junction soon after to field gate at 3.4m/5.5km. Go SO, turning L at T-junction with cairn at 0.6m/1km onto cairn-marked bridleway to Boot and keeping R at T-junction at 1m/1.6km to Bulatt Bridge by Burnmoor Tarn at 1.8m/2.9km. Go SO, forking R at cairn-marked T-junction at 0.5m/0.8km, ignoring farm track off L at 2.1m/3.4km, joining tarmac in Boot at 2.6m/4.2km and turning R at T-junction to start at 3.1m/5km.

SPORT Route 13
DUNNERDALE FELLS

Pivotal piece on this route's the Walna Scar road which is a riot of rocks and ruts courtesy of winter weather and MX bikes. Done as a descent it's fearsome, as an ascent it's plain intimidating — a push for most folk. Then there's the Lickle valley; the precipitous fellsides at its head frame fantastic views of the Duddon estuary with the Irish Sea beyond. Together with inspirational singletrack — best done as a descent — you're bound to want a return run. Try it in the opposite direction though — it'll be very different but exciting nonetheless.

DISTANCE
15 miles (24km)
HEIGHT-GAIN
2130ft (645m)
TIME
2.5hrs (dry)
4hrs (wet)
NAVIGATION SKILLS
moderate
RIDE DIRECTION
either way

Outdoor Leisure 6 The English Lakes SW

A tough loop this one but the rewards are rich. You're not likely to meet more varied riding over such a small area.

The Dunnerdale Fells are a magic mix of bare bedrock, twisting trails and sweeping fells.

❶ Start Ulpha car park (GR198920). Head N (towards Ulpha Bridge), taking hairpin turn R at 0.6m/1km up bridleway drive, going through gate onto forest track at 0.75m/1.2km, forking R at T-junction at 1.12m/1.8km and turning R up C-road at Kiln Bank at 2.1m/3.4km to X-roads with bridleway on summit at 2.7m/4.3km (optional start point). Turn L then immediately fork R (E) onto singletrack bridleway, going SO track at 0.2m/0.3km, climbing to turn L at T-junction above Stanton Ground at 1m/1.75km, swinging L (N) by wall at 1.5m/2.4km, crossing ford at 1.75m/2.8km then turning R onto grass-track at T-junction at 1.9m/3km to T-junction at Stephenson Ground at 2.2m/3.5km.

❷ Turn L, up Lickle valley, steep climb after ford then zigzagging R/L (effectively SO, N) at X-roads at 1.1m/1.75km, turning R (ENE then NNE) onto grass-track round rocky knoll at 1.3m/2.1km, rejoining obvious 'trail' at ford at 1.5m/2.4km, ignoring forks off R on descent to wall at 2.2m/3.5km which you follow to gated T-junction with Walna Scar Road at 2.4m/3.9km. Turn L through gate (descent gets very rocky; slippery when

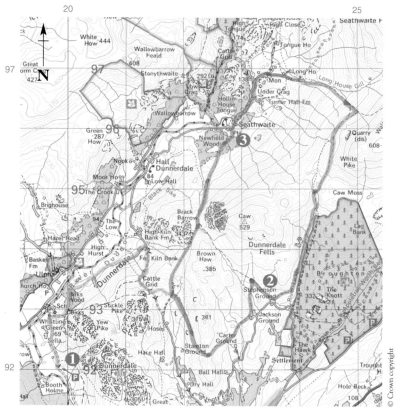

SPORT Route 13
DUNNERDALE FELLS

wet!), turning L onto unclassified road at 0.8m/1.3km and forking L onto C-road at 1.3m/2.1km, turning L on bridleway (on RH bend in Seathwaite) at 1.75m/2.8km up to go through gate at 1.8m/2.9km.

❸ Turn R (by wall), forking R (near sheepfold) at bridleway T-junction (in valley below Brock Barrow) at 1.12m/1.8km, keeping L at singletrack T-junction at 1.9m/3km, joining track at 1.9m/3.1km and turning L up singletrack at staggered X-roads at 2m/3.2km to C-road at 2.1m/3.4km. Turn R on outbound route to start at 2.7m/4.3km.

SPORT Route 14
PARKAMOOR AND GRIZEDALE

I last rode this in mid-winter after a heavy fall of snow and despite the bleak conditions the riding was excellent, the going good. So it's an ideal circuit for tough riders when the weather's closed in. In summer add the Satterthwaite loop to make an enjoyable, figure of eight Expert ride. Recent renovation has taken the terror out of descending the old road to Howe Head.

DISTANCE
18 miles (29km)
HEIGHT-GAIN
2410ft (730m)
TIME
3hrs (dry)
3.5hrs (wet)
NAVIGATION SKILLS
moderate
RIDE DIRECTION
anticlockwise

Outdoor Leisure 7 The English Lakes SE and 6 The English Lakes SW plus Pathfinder 626 Broughton in Furness & Newby Bridge

A classic Lakeland tour that'll take you up and away from the immensely popular Grizedale Forest fire-road circuits.

❶ Start Monk Coniston car park (GR316979; toilets here). Turn R, turning L up gated bridleway track at 0.75m/1.2km, going SO bridleway/track junction (into Grizedale Forest on singletrack) at Lawson Park at 2m/3.2km, turning R on forest track at 2.4m/3.9km and turning R on bridleway track (forest track turns L and is barred to cyclists) at 3m/4.8km to gate onto The Park moors at 3.7m/5.9km. Go SO (SW, on meandering, sometimes vague, singletrack), passing abandoned Low Parkamoor farm (on track) and swinging R at track T-junction at 1m/1.6km to T-junction with C-road at High Nibthwaite at 3m/4.8km (gate here!).

❷ Turn L, turning L at next T-junction at 1m/1.6km, climbing to keep SO at T-junction with Stock Farm bridleway at 1.8m/2.9km and keeping SO (signposted) on Ickenthwaite track at 1.9m/3.1km to gate at 2.25m/3.6km. Go SO (ENE, do not fork R), turning L at T-junction with C-road at High Ickenthwaite at 0.9m/1.4km, turning L at T-junction at 1.7m/2.75km, turning L on unclassified track at T-junction at 2.1m/3.4km, keeping SO at T-junction with C-road and turning L (on unclassified track) at T-junction at 2.9m/4.6km and R up singletrack at 3.6m/5.7km to forest road at 3.6m/5.75km.

SPORT Route 14 PARKAMOOR AND GRIZEDALE

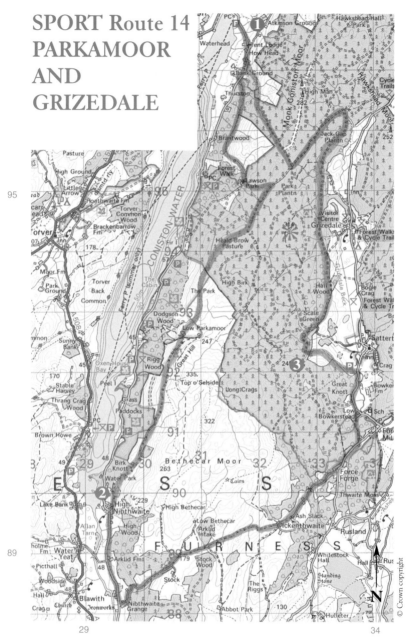

❸ Turn R (N, on forest road that keeps close to forest edge), forking L at T-junction at 1.1m/1.75km and turning L at track T-junction at 2.7m/4.3km up to staggered X-roads at 3.6m/5.75km. Turn R (NW), forking L at T-junction at 0.3m/0.5km (on Monk Coniston Moor), forking L at T-junction with unclassified track at 0.5m/0.8km (just past wall end), descending to C-road at 1.2m/1.9km (How Head) and turning R on outbound route to start at 1.7m/2.75km.

FUN Route 15
SATTERTHWAITE

① Start Blind Lane car park and picnic site (GR344913) near Force Mills. Turn R (W, towards Force Mills) and turning R at T-junction (towards Satterthwaite) at 0.25m/0.4km to T-junction with forest road at Bogle Crag picnic site at 4.1m/6.6km. Turn R, going SO at T-junction at 0.4m/0.6km, keeping R at T-junction at 1.4m/2.2km (on hairpin at valley head, effectively SO) and swinging R over spur to T-junction with singletrack bridleway off L (E) at 1.8m/2.9km.

② Go 75yds/70m, going SO through tall gate, through two fords (on twisty singletrack then fire-road), turning L at T-junction at 0.5m/0.8km, passing tall log sculpture (Cathedral of Unknown Desires) and turning L on way-marked bridleway at 0.6m/1km down to C-road at 0.9m/1.5km. Turn R, turning L on bridleway track 100yds/90m, swinging R (NE) in field at 0.15m/0.25km and going through gate into woods at 0.2m/0.3km on obvious single-track to C-road at Devil's Gallop at 0.8m/1.3km. Turn R, turning R at T-junction with bridleway at Hazleseat at1.4m/2.2km, turning R at path/track junction onto bridle-way singletrack at 2.25m/3.6km, turning L on C-road at Low Dale Park at 3m/4.8km and keeping R at T-junctions soon after to start at 3.5m/5.6km.

DISTANCE
9 miles (15km)
HEIGHT-GAIN
1185ft (360m)
TIME
2hrs (dry)
3hrs (wet)
NAVIGATION
SKILLS
moderate
RIDE DIRECTION
clockwise

Outdoor Leisure 7
The English Lakes
SE

There's plenty of scope for enjoying the marked mountain bike routes in Grizedale Forest but the original bridle-ways are definitely more entertaining. So expect a bit of rough 'n tumble, stump jumping and bog-trots on this loop as well as the usual forest fire-road fare.

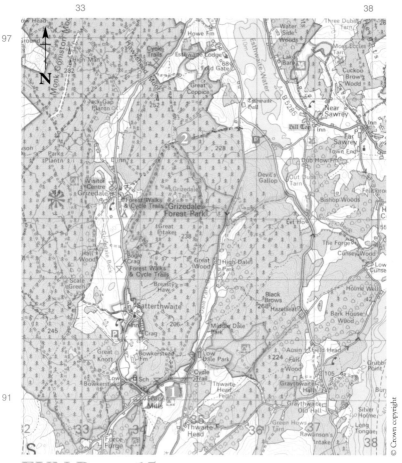

FUN Route 15
SATTERTHWAITE

CENTRAL LAKELAND

Loughrigg Terrace overlooking Grasmere (Route 16)

SPORT Route 16
LANGDALE AND LOUGHRIGG

DISTANCE
17 miles (27km)
HEIGHT-GAIN
2130ft (645m)
TIME
2.5hrs (dry)
3hrs (wet)
NAVIGATION
SKILLS
easy
RIDE DIRECTION
either way

Outdoor Leisure 7
The English Lakes
SE

An AC/DC route much favoured by local bikers that would make an excellent night ride.

The underlying terrain is craggy, wrinkled rock criss-crossed by mine access tracks, footpaths, by-ways and bustling, traffic-carrying roads. Be extra vigilant on these; the Ambleside/Grasmere area is a tourist hot-spot, even the smallest lanes are busy and holiday motorists' eyes are frequently drawn to the breath-taking scenery. And it's the intimate contact with this scenery that makes this route so special — that and the thrilling ride.

It's all low-level — we're never more than 875ft (265m) up — in Lake District terms but the route's a tortuous one with different vistas at every turn and the intervening trail spiced up by an ad hoc mix of ambling and exhilaration. It begs to be ridden fast and therein lies the rub — line of sight is restricted and the whole place is chocka with tourists. Especially Loughrigg Terrace! Pushchairs perambulating along the mining tracks in the Langdales are common in summer. Your best bet is to select a time-slot well outside the usual tourist hours of 10-to-6 or use it as a bad weather alternative to more adventurous mountain routes.

❶ Start Miller Bridge, Loughrigg Lane (GR371045). Turn R (N, towards Rydal), immediately turning L up tarmac bridleway immediately after cattle-grid, going through gate at 0.9m/1.5km, singletrack swings R at 1.4m/2.2km, going SO track X-roads at 1.9m/3km and keeping L in Tarn Foot at 1.9m/3.1km to C-road at 2m/3.15km. Zigzag R/L (steep descent to junction!), going SO on A593 over Skelwith Bridge (tea-room on R) soon after, turning L through gate up finger-posted bridle-way (towards Arnside) at 1.12m/1.8km and swinging L after going through gap in wall (near Arnside) at 1.9m/3km up to gate at 2.3m/3.7km (turn round for view!).

❷ Go SO, into forest, turning R on BOAT at signed T-junction at 0.6m/0.9km, keeping L on tarmac at 1.6m/2.5km, turning R on A593 soon after and turning L on tarmac bridleway at 1.7m/2.75km to gate at High Oxen Fell farm. Go SO (on track), swinging L through Hodge Close (seasonal tea-room here) hamlet at 0.4m/0.6km, forking R (on track) at T-junction at 0.4m/0.7km, going SO X-roads at 0.6m/1km and keeping R (towards Little Langdale) at signed T-junc-

tion at 0.75m/1.2km to footbridge at 1.3m/2.1km. Go over bridge (ford is deep!), turning L on C-road at 0.4m/0.6km and turning R up waymarked unclassified road at 0.6m/0.9km to gate at 1.25m/2km.

❸ Go through gate, immediately forking L down bridleway single-track (rough in places), turning R on track at 0.25m/0.4km, zigzagging L/R (on signed bridleway) across track soon after, following signs through quarry, keeping L at

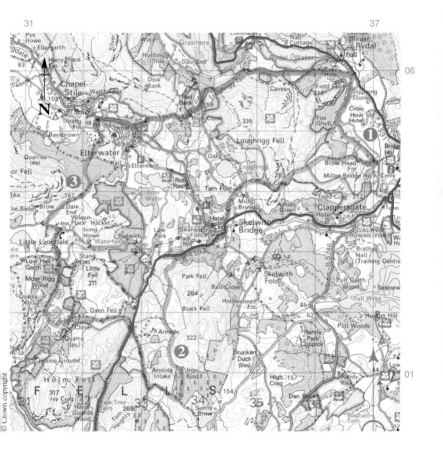

0.5m/0.75km, keeping R at T-junction at 0.5m/0.8km and turning L (over footbridge) at 0.7m/1.1km to B5343 by Wainwright's Inn. Turn R, turning L (up C-road) at 0.4m/0.6km, turning R at T-junction at 0.5m/0.8km (optional off-road climb off R at 0.6m/1km), turning L at T-junction (beyond High Close YHA) at 1.25m/2km and forking R (down bridleway) at 1.3m/2.15km to gate at 1.4m/2.25km. NOTE: next section down Loughrigg Terrace is a very popular walk — please take extra care. Swing R, rough chicane at 0.4m/0.6km, keeping R to go through gate at 1.12m/1.8km and turning R at T-junction with C-road at 1.6m/2.6km to start at 2.7m/4.3km.

EXPERT Route 17
AMBLESIDE TO LONGSLEDDALE VIA GARBURN PASS

We start with the cruel, gut-busting climb past Jenkin Crag. Garburn Pass, high point of the route, is being 'improved' with annual sessions of repair work so if you like it rough don't delay. Famed sections of endo track are fast disappearing under swathes of paving slabs.

Mags Howe tea-rooms, situated in Green Quarter above Kentmere, are an obligatory stop and an ideal place to stay too. After that there's an entertaining track ride over to Sleddale and an even more entertaining session of singletracking on the return leg to Kentmere. Take care with the navigation, especially if the weather's closed in, or you might end up in Staveley. The last off-road blast, down to the main road back into Ambleside, is a touch rubbly and a bit skippy if wet.

DISTANCE
28 miles (45km)
HEIGHT-GAIN
3810ft (1155m)
TIME
5.5hrs (dry)
7hrs (wet)
NAVIGATION
SKILLS
moderate
RIDE DIRECTION
as shown

Outdoor Leisure 7
The English Lakes
SE

Penned out by local bikers in Ambleside this meandering route is centred on the renowned Coast-to-Coast off-road ride as it heads east toward Shap.

❶ Start Waterhead car park (GR377039, off A591) and turn R (S, towards Windermere), taking hairpin turn L at 0.12m/0.2km, taking hairpin turn R (up tarmac bridleway towards Troutbeck) at 0.2m/0.3km, forking L at singletrack T-junction at 0.6m/1km (trail splits soon, keep L for rideable climb) and going through High Skelghyll farm to bridleway/drive T-junction at 1.4m/2.3km. Turn L through gate (towards Troutbeck), turning R (by seat) at track T-junction at 0.8m/1.3km, turning L on C-road, soon forking R down bridleway at 1.2m/1.9km and going SO C-road in Town End to A592 at 1.5m/2.4km.

❷ Turn R, almost immediately turning L on C-road, turning L on Dubbs Lane track (No Through Road, BOAT) at T-junction at 1.25m/2km and keeping R at T-junc-

tion at 3m/4.75km to gate just over Garburn Pass at 4.4m/7.1km. Go SO (rocky descent with roughly paved sections) into Kentmere, turning L at C-road T-junction (immediately after bridge) at 1.6m/2.6km, turning L at next T-junction (tea-rooms in Green Quarter, 0.12m/0.2km — turn R here, next L and up tarmac drive) and turning R (towards Sadgill) up BOAT track at 2.5m/4km (limited lay-by parking here) to signed, gated T-junction at 3.75m/6km (immediately after tricky zigzag descent).

❸ Turn R (through ford), soon swinging R (up grass singletrack), going SO waymarked X-roads at 1.6m/2.5km on Green Quarter Fell and swinging L through gate at 1.9m/3km to swing L through field gate at 2.5m/4km. Go SO (on track at first), turning R through gate at bridleway T-junction (not waymarked) at 100yds/90m, going SO vague X-roads at 0.25m/0.4km, swinging R at 0.4m/0.6km, turning L by waymarkers at 0.75m/1.2km and 0.8m/1.3km down to C-road at 1.1m/1.7km. Turn L, turning R on bridleway at 0.2m/0.3km, keeping R (on gated, stony bridleway) immediately after Ullthwaite Bridge, keep-

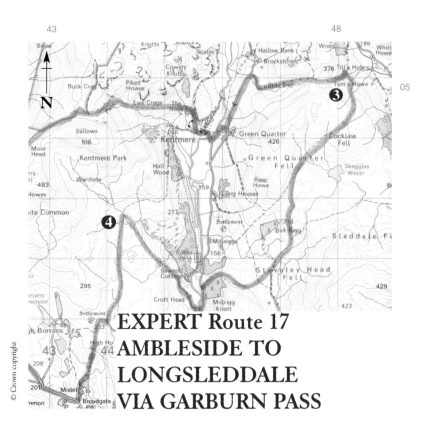

EXPERT Route 17
AMBLESIDE TO
LONGSLEDDALE
VIA GARBURN PASS

ing L at T-junction with footpath at 0.5m/0.75km and going SO through ford/gate combo at 0.9m/1.5km to singletrack T-junction just before gate at 1.6m/2.6km.

❹ Take hairpin turn L (over stream on singletrack bridleway), turning R (towards High House) at gated T-junction at 1.25m/2km, soon swinging L on bridleway track, through High House farm, turning R on C-road at 2.2m/3.5km, keeping R at T-junction soon after, going SO at staggered X-roads at 2.6m/4.2km and going SO at next T-junction to familiar T-junction with Dubbs

Lane track at 3.4m/5.5km. Fork R (No Through Road), taking hairpin turn L at T-junction at 1.7m/2.75km, going SO staggered track X-roads at 2.1m/3.3km, turning R on A592, turning L (towards Troutbeck) at 2.6m/4.2km, turning L at next T-junction and keeping R at T-junction at 3.25m/5.2km to finger-posted T-junction with bridleway track at 3.6m/5.7km. Fork L, keeping R at track T-junction at 0.15m/0.25km (a bit rubbly in places), swinging R at 0.6m/1km and turning R on A591 (busy road!) at 1m/1.6km into Ambleside and the start at 3.25m/5.2km.

Carry to Garburn pass, Kentmere (Route 17) ...

SOUTH EASTERN LAKELAND

... and a rocky descent to Troutbeck

FUN Route 18
KENTMERE VALLEY

DISTANCE
12.5miles (20km)
HEIGHT-GAIN
1355ft (410m)
TIME
2hrs (dry)
2.5hrs (wet)
NAVIGATION
SKILLS
easy
RIDE DIRECTION
clockwise

Outdoor Leisure 7
The English Lakes
SE

Easy to find your way around this mix and match of track, singletrack and lane which is ideal for young teenage 'wannabees' to test their mettle on. Take care on the last drop into Kentmere Valley — it gets a might cobbly!

When Windermere and the Central Lakes are all chocka with bumblies and what you really need are pedestrian-free trails to explore then head for this circuit in the Kentmere valley.

❶ Start west end of Dane Road, Staveley (GR461984). Head W (towards Windermere) on cycleway alongside A591, turning R up dead-end-road (opposite Ings; caf here) at 1.1m/1.7km, joining bridleway track at 1.4m/2.3km, going SO at T-junction at 2.3m/3.7km and turning R (towards Kentmere) at gated T-junction at 2.7m/4.25km to gated bridleway T-junction at 3.9m/6.25km. Go SO, keeping by wall on R, soon joining track to Kentmere Hall, turning R on C-road at 1.75m/2.8km and taking hairpin turn L at 2.1m/3.3km up to signed bridleway at 2.4m/3.8km in Green Quarter. NOTE: keep SO up lane for 150yds/135m for tea-rooms.

❷ Take hairpin turn R through gate (towards Cocklaw), turning L at waymarked T-junction at 0.2m/0.3km, swinging L at 0.9m/1.4km, going SO through gate at 1m/1.6km and turning R at waymarked X-roads at 1.3m/2.1km on singletrack to gate at 1.6m/2.6km. Go SO through gate, keeping L through gate at 0.6m/1km on track, turning R through gate at bridleway T-junction (not waymarked) at 0.7m/1.1km, going SO vague X-roads at 0.9m/1.4km, swinging R at 1m/1.6km, turning L by waymarkers at 1.4m/2.2km and 1.4m/2.3km down to C-road at 1.7m/2.75km.

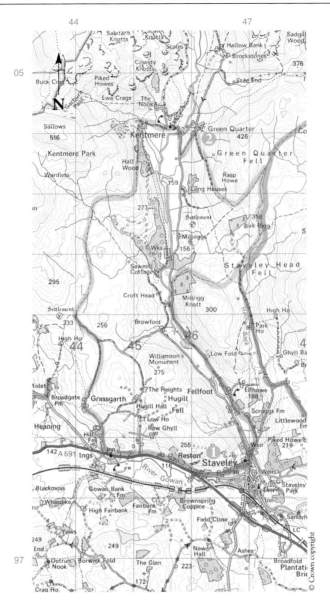

© Crown copyright

Turn L, forking L on finger-posted bridleway at 1.25m/2km, through Scroggs farm, turning R on C-road at 1.8m/2.9km, turning R over bridge then L at staggered X-roads at 1.9m/3.1km, turning R at T-junction by church at 2m/3.25km (on Brow Lane) and turning R (on Dane Road) at 2.4m/3.8km to start at 2.7m/4.25km.

SPORT Route 19
SLEDDALE FOREST CIRCUIT

DISTANCE
17 miles (27km)
HEIGHT-GAIN
1850ft (560m)
TIME
2.5hrs (dry)
3.5hrs (wet)
NAVIGATION
SKILLS
moderate
RIDE DIRECTION
anticlockwise

Outdoor Leisure 7
The English Lakes
SE

A good introduction to mountain biking this loop's a blend of typical English off-road fare: farm lanes, fields, ancient moorland byways, sinuous singletrack and rocky cart track.

There's room to draw off the road beyond the gate near Piked Howe farm but it's not popular with the locals so you're as well to start off in Staveley. The back road from Staveley to Garnett Bridge undulates gently and there are fine views across lowland Cumbria. An excellent way to warm up but before you get to the tough stuff there's an extended session of gate keeping for a few miles up Long Sleddale. It's a bit of a pain and there's a quiet lane on a parallel path but the off-road route is on old track for the most part and affords some memorable views of the Dale. That makes the effort worthwhile. Once you've conquered the climb out of Sleddale — a push in parts for most folk — the fun begins on a bleak bit of moor but there's an excellent, semi-technical, singletrack bridleway that cuts right across it. Mind the black bog holes — some are deep, some are not — and the bends as you descend from Birk Rigg. All that pell-mell singletracking winds down on track then tarmac to the finish.

❶ Start at bridleway T-junction with gated road at Piked Howe (GR483989). From gate turn L (SSE) on finger-posted bridleway, going SO waymarked X-roads soon after (can be overgrown here), swinging L on to tarmac at 0.3m/0.5km, turning L on C-road at 0.6m/1km, taking hairpin turn L at next T-junction, turning L at T-junction at 4.6m/7.3km and turning L on track in Garnett Bridge at 5.4m/8.6km to gate at 5.5m/8.8km. Go SO through gate, swinging R then L at 0.12m/0.2km, going through (towards Nether House) bridle-gate at 0.2m/0.3km, climbing R and going SO after gate in field corner at 0.3m/0.5km across field to farm drive track at 0.6m/1km.

❷ Fork L, forking R through gate just after Bridge End farm at 0.7m/1.1km, across field, through gate at 0.9m/1.5km and immediately turning L on track, turning L on grass-track at finger-posted T-junction at 1.12m/1.8km, swinging L through gate at 1.3m/2.1km and going SO X-roads by Kilnstones farm on old grass-track to gated T-junction with waymarker at 2.1m/3.3km. Swing L, swinging R then L after gate at 80yds/75m, passing waymarker, zigzagging R/L past Wads Howe farm at 0.4m/0.7km, going SO bridleway X-

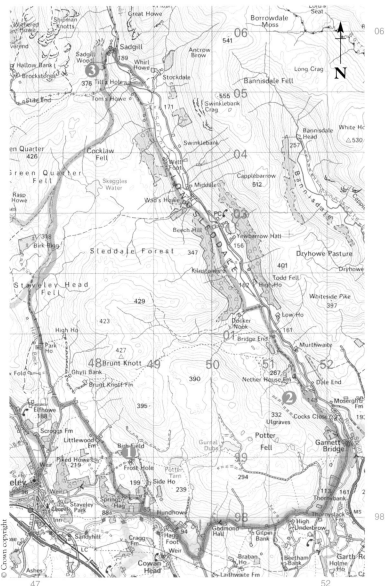

roads at 0.7m/1.1km, forking L at waymarked, gated junction at 0.8m/1.3km (round Well Foot farm) and going SO on concrete bridleway at T-junction at 1.6m/2.5km to gate by Tom's Howe at 1.7m/2.75km. Fork R through gate, turning R on bridleway drive at 0.15m/0.25km, turning L on C-road soon after, turning L on BOAT track at T-junction in Sadgill at 0.75m/1.2km and turning L immediately after bridge up track to gated T-junction with bridleway at 1.25m/2km.

❸ Turn L (through ford), soon swinging R (up grass singletrack), going SO waymarked X-roads at 1.6m/2.5km on Green Quarter Fell and on to gate at 1.9m/3km. Go SO through gate, keeping L through gate at 0.6m/1km on track then tarmac, forking L at T-junction at 2m/3.2km, turning R at T-junction soon after and passing through gate at Littlewood farm to start at 3m/4.8km.

HOWGILL FELLS

Bowderdale in the Howgills (Route 20)

EXPERT Route 20
LUNE VALLEY LOOP

DISTANCE
32 miles (52km)
HEIGHT-GAIN
4785ft (1450m)
TIME
5hrs (dry)
7hrs (wet)
NAVIGATION
SKILLS
moderate
RIDE DIRECTION
anticlockwise

Outdoor Leisure 7
The English Lakes
SE and 19 The
Howgill Fells

*Many bikers will have
looked longingly at the
precipitous slopes of
the Howgill Fells as
they sped by, hammer-
ing along the M6
where it squeezes past
Tebay in the Lune
valley. Few will have
stopped to go riding in
them there hills. Next
time don't ignore the
call and go ride
this loop.*

A little east of Tebay and Orton lies Bowderdale —
Bowderdale has one the best sections of singletrack
in Cumbria. Period. And a stone's throw west is
Borrowdale. Not the famed valley in the heart of
the Lakes, no, this precipitous little dale is altogeth-
er more intimate but sports some outstanding trails.
Our route links the two with a loop across the upper
Lune valley. Orton is a good spot to start with a
shop and excellent tea rooms on hand — there are
no refuelling facilities on the ride — along with a
convenient inn that caters for C-t-C hikers. Radical
riding doesn't start until you get into Bowderdale.
Then it's singletrack right through the heart of the
Howgills. Singletrack that gets progressively more
technical as it climbs. And you can ride the lot
including the climb if you're strong enough! There's
no right of access to the trig on top of The Calf but,
as every obvious route on the hill heads for it, you'll
probably end up there. To rejoin the Route head
north-west for 200m down a well-used path; a vague
singletrack joining from the east marks your return
to the bridleway. Whilst on top you'll be treated to
a coast-to-coast panorama if it's clear then you're in
for a pell-mell run down White Fell. In the wet the
grass and slate's as slippery as eel skin which, with
an 800ft drop immediately off left, makes for an
exciting ride. Watch out for the rutted chicanes
near the bottom though! A mix of track and lane
takes you to the transmitting station on the rim of
Borrowdale (here you have to take care to pick the
right descent) for another session of rough 'n tum-
ble biking — two radical downhill runs and a calf-
stretching ascent — then it's a short wind-down
along the lanes back into Orton.

❶ Start Orton village centre car park (GR622082) and head S on the B6260 (towards Tebay), soon turning L on B6261 (towards Kirkby Stephen), turning R at 0.6m/1km (towards Gaisgill), turning L on public byway at 1.7m/2.75km (signed Wain Gap), at track end turning R on C-road, turning L (towards Kirkby Stephen) at T-junction soon after, taking hairpin turn R (towards Wath) at 5.3m/8.5km and forking R at T-junction at 5.7m/9.1km to T-junction with finger-posted bridleway track at 6.25m/10km.

❷ Turn L, swinging R after 2nd gate and forking L at track T-junction at 0.5m/0.75km and swinging L at 0.9m/1.4km round wall on single-track up Bowderdale to carry across Rams Gill at 3.9m/6.3km (just before big climb). Climb obvious singletrack, forking R at 1m/1.6km on vague bridleway (W then WSW; easy to miss; if you end up at trig turn R and you'll rejoin route 200m WNW), forking R at T-junction at 1.6m/2.5km to follow obvious singletrack swinging L right round rim of Calf Beck head, keeping L at vague T-junction at 2m/3.2km on White Fell Head (steep descent; very slippery when wet; track near bottom is rough!) and swinging L across Chapel Beck at 3.1m/4.9km up to gate at 3.6m/5.75km.

❸ Go through gate, soon swinging R on Castley Farm drive, going SO C-road X-roads at 0.6m/1km (opt-out: turn R here to A685 at the mouth of Borrowdale), zigzagging R/L across B6257 (towards Lambrigg) at 1.8m/2.9km, turning R (towards Grayrigg) at 2.4m/3.8km, turning R at T-junction at 3.3m/5.3km, turning L on A685 at 3.9m/6.25km and turning R in Grayrigg (towards Whinfell) at 4.6m/7.4km to X-roads with tracks at 5.8m/9.3km at Deepslack. Turn R through gate up concrete bridleway to T-junction with bridleway grass-track at 1.8m/2.9km (not signed; it's immediately after passing 1st mast).

❹ Fork L (ENE), swinging L at 0.6m/0.9km down zigzag track, turning L up Low Borrowdale Farm drive at 0.9m/1.5km, zigzagging R/L (effectively SO up Borrowdale) through farm at 2.3m/3.7km and forking R at T-junction at 2.6m/4.1km to bridleway public byway staggered X-roads at 4.25m/6.8km. Turn R, over Borrow Beck (up Breasthigh Road), keeping R at T-junction at 1.12m/1.8km, turning R on tarmac byway at 1.6m/2.5km, keeping R at Midwath T-junction at 2.1m/3.3km, turning L at next T-junction and turning R at Greenholme at 3.75m/6km to follow signs to Orton and start at 5.9m/9.5km.

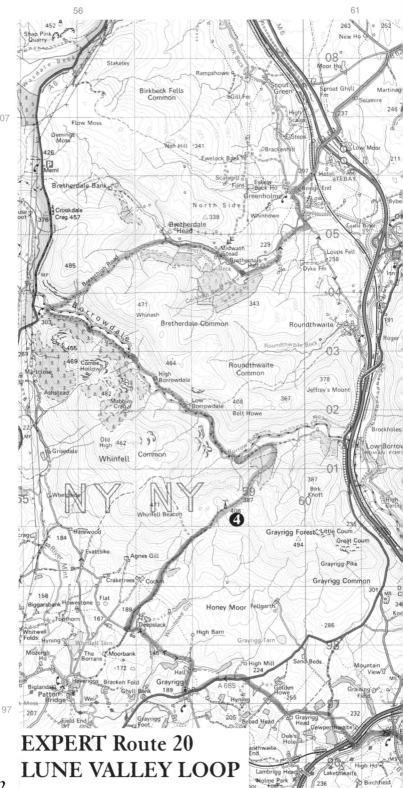

EXPERT Route 20
LUNE VALLEY LOOP

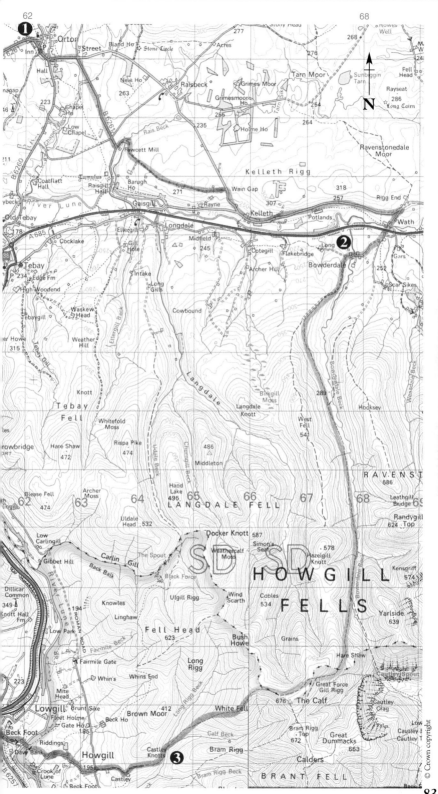

SPORT Route 21
GREAT ASBY SCARS

DISTANCE
21 miles (34km)
HEIGHT-GAIN
2000ft (605m)
TIME
2.5hrs (dry)
3.5hrs (wet)
NAVIGATION
SKILLS
easy
RIDE DIRECTION
either way

Outdoor Leisure 19
The Howgill Fells

Striking circuit across the lunar landscape of Great Asby Scar — the UK's most impressive limestone pavement — plus a pootle on The Coast to Coast mountain bike ride's most pastoral part. Not a wet weather route.

A sort of "no-man's land" east of Orton Great Asby Scars and Smardale Gill valley is rarely visited by mountain bikers. So this is a loop for seekers of solitude. A mix of by-way, lanes and abandoned main road serves as an easy intro to the route. Off-road escapades begin in earnest at Brownber when pastoral tracks take you to an old packhorse bridge across Smardale Beck. Upstream is the impressive Scandal Beck Viaduct. This is where the easy-going cart track turns technical and, with gravity on the opposing team, it's a tough climb onto Smardale Fell before a downhill run across fields to the Hall. On a clockwise run you can do a short detour east to avoid a grinder climb over grass.

This mix-and-match of ambling and rough stuff is typical of the loop and the technical bits will catch you off-guard. Especially the rock-stops and roots on the sunk lane out of Crosby Garrett. Not white-knuckle but definitely a tease. Soon after our loop hooks up with the C-t-C mountain bike route past Masongill for a bit of farm track and field riding. Cattle-mashed gateways get mega-gloopy in the wet so be prepared for mud! Luckily it's soon over and we're back to track and singletrack over Great Asby Scars - an awesome bit of scenery — before the final pell-mell run to the road east of Orton. Last one to the tea-room buys the buns!

❶ Start Orton village centre car park (GR622082) and head S on the B6260 (towards Tebay), soon turning L on B6261 (towards Kirkby Stephen), turning R at 0.6m/1km (towards Gaisgill), turning L on public by-way at 1.7m/2.75km (signed Wain Gap), at track end turning R on C-road, turning L (towards Kirkby Stephen) at T-junction soon after and turning L (towards Great Asby) at T-junction at 6.6m/10.5km to X-roads with gated bridleways (not signed) at 6.75m/10.8km.

❷ Turn R, over cattle-grid on track/tarmac through Brownber (dogs!), going SO at all junctions, zigzagging L/R (Effectively SO) at staggered X-roads at Friar's Bottom Farm at 0.6m/1km, swinging L through gate at 0.8m/1.3km, over Smardale Bridge and keeping L (towards Smardale) alongside wall at bridleway X-roads at 2.3m/3.75km to C-road T-junction at 3.3m/5.3km. Turn L and immediately turning L (towards Crosby Garrett) again, zigzagging L/R (Effectively SO) in village at 1.2m/1.9km, forking L on track over Settle-Carlisle line at 1.5m/2.4km and forking L off main track at 1.6m/2.5km (rocky and gets over-grown) to bridle-gate immediately after sharp L bend at 2.2m/3.5km.

❸ Go through gate, going SO field, turning R on gated track at 0.25m/0.4km, turning L on C-road at 1.3m/2.1km and swinging R at Whygill Head X-roads (towards Great Asby) for 50yds/50m up to gated bridleway. Turn L through gate (towards Maisongill on way-marked bridleway), swinging R across field (gets muddy), zigzagging by 100yds/90m L/R at 0.4m/0.6km and turning L on Asby Grange drive at 0.9m/1.5km to gate on corner at 1.12m/1.8km. Go through gate on waymarked bridleway, joining Maisongill Farm drive at 0.75m/1.2km, turning L on C-road at 1.6m/2.5km and turning L on bridleway track (not signed) at 1.9m/3km to 2nd gate at 2.6m/4.2km.

❹ Go through gate, forking R off grass-track soon after, up through bridle-gate at 0.1m/0.15km (English Nature Reserve, please ride with care), keeping L on singletrack by wall, swinging R at 0.2m/0.3km, zigzagging L/R on bit of track at 0.7m/1.1km and climbing to go over stile by ENR sign at 0.9m/1.5km. Go SO (singletrack gets a bit vague), swinging L through bridle-gate at 0.25m/0.4km, soon joining rough track paralleling wall and turning R on C-road at 1.5m/2.4km back to Orton at 2.6m/4.2km.

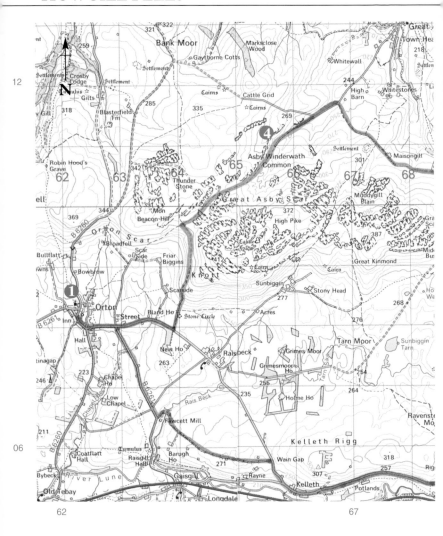

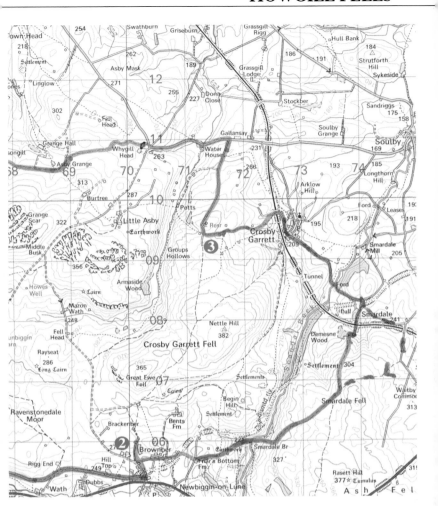

SPORT Route 21
GREAT ASBY SCARS

C-t-C territory near Scandal Beck, Ravenstonedale (Route 21)

APPENDICES

WEATHER NEWS

Lake District in detail	☎ 01768 775757
Cumbria Weathercall	☎ 0891 500 419
Mountaincall	☎ 0891 500 483

TOURIST INFORMATION CENTRES

Appleby-in-Westmorland	☎ 017683 51177
Carlisle	☎ 01228 512444
Cockermouth	☎ 01900 822634
Egremont	☎ 01946 820693
Kendal	☎ 01539 725758
Keswick	☎ 01768 772645
Penrith	☎ 01768 674666
Sellafield	☎ 019467 27021
Southwaite	☎ 016974 73445/6
Windermere	☎ 015394 47439

YOUTH HOSTELS

Ambleside, Waterhead	☎ 01 5394 32304	Central Lakes
Black Sail Hut (upper Ennerdale)		NW Lakes
Borrowdale	☎ 017687 77257	NW Lakes
Buttermere	☎ 017687 70245	NW Lakes
Carrock Fell	☎ 016974 78325	NE Lakes
Coniston Copper Mines	☎ 015394 41261	SW Lakes
Coniston	☎ 015394 41323	SW Lakes
Derwent Water	☎ 017687 77246	NW Lakes
Elterwater	☎ 015394 37245	Central Lakes
Ennerdale	☎ 01946 861237	NW Lakes
Eskdale, Boot	☎ 019467 23219	SW Lakes
Grasmere, Butterlip How	☎ 015394 35316	Central Lakes
Grasmere, Thorney How	☎ 015394 35591	Central Lakes
Hawkshead	☎ 015394 36293	SW Lakes

Helvellyn, Patterdale	☎ 017684 82269	NE Lakes
Honister Hause	☎ 017687 77267	NW Lakes
Kendal	☎ 01539 724066	SE Lakes
Keswick	☎ 017687 72484	NE Lakes
Langdale	☎ 015394 37313	Central Lakes
Langdale, Loughrigg	☎ 015394 37313	Central Lakes
Patterdale	☎ 017684 82394	NE Lakes
Skiddaw	☎ 016974 78325	NE Lakes
Tebay	☎ 015396 24286	SE Lakes/Howgills
Thirlmere	☎ 017687 73224	NE Lakes
Wastwater	☎ 019467 26222	SW Lakes
Windermere, Troutbeck	☎ 015394 43543	SE Lakes

YOUTH HOSTELS ASSOCIATION

Trevelyan House, 8 St Stephen's Hill, St Albans, Herts AL1 2DY
☎ 0101727 855215

YHA Northern England Region ☎ 0101629 824571

BIKE SHOPS

NE Lakes

Keswick Mountain Bikes	☎ 01768 775202
The Lakeland Pedlar, Bell Close, Keswick	☎ 01768 775752
Arragon Cycles, 2 Brunswick Road, Penrith	☎ 01768 890344
Scotby Cycles, Carlisle	☎ 01228 46931

Western Lakes

Halfords, Whitehaven	☎ 01900 604615

Central Lakes

Bike Treks, 2 Millans Park, Ambleside	☎ 015394 31245
Ghyllside Cycles, The Slack, Ambleside	☎ 015394 33592

SE Lakes

Wheelbase, Staveley	☎ 01539 821443
Lakeland Leisure, Station Precinct, Windermere	☎ 015394 44786
Ashtons Windermere Cycles, Windermere	☎ 015394 47779

BRITISH RAIL BOOKING INFORMATION   ☎ 0345 484950

Stations are located at: Carlisle, Kendal, Penrith, Ravenglass, St Bees, Staveley, Whitehaven, Windermere

LAKE DISTRICT NATIONAL PARK   ☎ 019662 6601

Lake District Nat Pk, Brockhole, Windermere, Cumbria LA23 1LJ

CUMBRIA COUNTY COUNCIL

Highways & Transportation, County Offices, Kendal, Cumbria LA9 4RG

FOREST ENTERPRISE   ☎ 01229 860373

Lakes Forest District, Grizedale, Hawkshead, Ambleside, Cumbria LA22 0QJ.

THE CYCLISTS TOURING CLUB

Since 1878 the Cyclists Touring Club (CTC) has been the governing body for recreational cycling in this country and is recognised by such organisations as the Sports Council, the Department of Transport and the Department of the Environment. Membership is open to anyone interested in cycling. They currently have 40000+ members, 200 nationwide clubs and 100 local clubs affiliated to them.

Recently the CTC has taken on responsibility for addressing off-road cycling access issues which includes promoting Rights of Way initiatives wherever they occur and representing the views of mountain bikers at local and national levels. Local representation is done through a network of volunteer Access Officers.

If you would like to apply for membership then please apply to: CTC, Dept CSB/94, 69 Meadrow, Godalming, Surrey GU7 3HS. ☎ 01483 417217.

Benefits of being a member include: representation on Rights of Way and access issues in your area, 3rd Party insurance cover, free legal advice for cycling related problems, free legal aid, free technical advice, free international touring info, bi-monthly colour magazine, free handbook, mail order service and a voice in the world of MTBing.

OTHER DALESMAN TITLES

Mountain Biking
MOUNTAIN BIKE ROUTE GUIDE: YORKSHIRE DALES
Tim Woodcock £7.99

Walking and Trail Guides
LAKE DISTRICT, WESTERN FELLS Paddy Dillon £5.99
LAKE DISTRICT, EASTERN FELLS Paddy Dillon £5.99
YORKSHIRE DALES, SOUTH & WESTERN AREA
Terry Marsh £5.99
YORKSHIRE DALES, NORTH & EASTERN AREA
Terry Marsh £5.99
WHITE PEAK Martin Smith £4.99
DARK PEAK John Gillham £4.99
NORTH PENNINES Alan Hall £4.99
SOUTH PENNINES John Gillham £4.99
LANCASHIRE John Gillham £4.99
NORTH YORK MOORS Nick Channer £4.99
CLEVELAND WAY Martin Collins £4.99
COAST TO COAST Ronald Turnbull £4.99
PENNINE WAY Terry Marsh £4.99

Walks Around Series
BAKEWELL Martin Smith £1.99
BUXTON Andrew McCloy £1.99
CASTLETON John Gillham £1.99
MATLOCK Martin Smith £1.99
AMBLESIDE Tom Bowker £1.99
HAWKSHEAD Mary Welsh £1.99
KESWICK Dawn Gibson £1.99
WINDERMERE Robert Gambles £1.99
GRASSINGTON Richard Musgrave £1.99
SETTLE & MALHAM Richard Musgrave £1.99

HAWES Richard Musgrave £1.99

RICHMOND Richard Musgrave £1.99

PICKERING Nick Channer £1.99

WHITBY Nick Channer £1.99

KIRKBYMOORSIDE Nick Channer £1.99

HELMSLEY Nick Channer £1.99

Pub Walks Series

LAKE DISTRICT Terry Marsh £5.99

NORTH YORK MOORS & COAST

Richard Musgrave £5.99

PEAK DISTRICT John Morrison £5.99

LANCASHIRE Terry Marsh £5.99

YORKSHIRE DALES Richard Musgrave £5.95

Dalesman Tea Shop Walks Series

LAKE DISTRICT Mary Welsh 5.99

YORKSHIRE DALES Richard Musgrave £5.95

PEAK DISTRICT Andrew McCloy £5.99

Safety for Walkers

MOUNTAIN SAFETY Kevin Walker £4.99

MAP READING Robert Matkin £3.50

Available from all good bookshops.

For a full list of Dalesman titles contact

Dalesman Publishing Company, Stable Courtyard,

Broughton Hall, Skipton, North Yorkshire, BD23 3AZ.

Tel: 01756 701381 • Fax: 01756 701381

web: http//www.dalesman.co.uk